CHILDREN OF THE SAME GOD

CHILDREN OF THE SAME GOD

The Historical Relationship Between Unitarianism, Judaism, and Islam

Susan J. Ritchie

Skinner House Books
Boston

www.skinnerhouse.org

Printed in the United States

Cover and text design by Suzanne Morgan

print ISBN: 978-1-55896-725-0
eBook ISBN: 978-1-55896-726-7

6 5 4 3 2 1
16 15 14

Library of Congress Cataloging-in-Publication Data

Ritchie, Susan, 1966-
Children of the same God : the historical relationship between Unitarianism, Judaism, and Islam / Susan J. Ritchie.
    pages cm
  Includes bibliographical references and index.
  ISBN 978-1-55896-725-0 (pbk. : alk. paper)—ISBN 978-1-55896-726-7 (ebook)
  1. Unitarianism—History. 2. Unitarianism—Relations—Judaism. 3. Judaism—Relations—Unitarianism. 4. Unitarianism—Relations—Islam. 5. Islam—Relations—Unitarianism. I. Title.
  BX9831.R58 2014
  289.109—dc23
                                                              2013034494

We gratefully acknowledge permission to print the photo of the ruins of the Catholic church in Bozodujfala, taken by Suzi Spandenberg.

The cover image shows the detail of a nave mosaic in The Basilica of Sant' Apollinare Nuovo in Ravenna, Italy. Created in about 500 CE, the mosaic depicts the palace of Theodoric, an Arian king. Arian Christians believed that Jesus was created by God, rather than co-equal with God. While such views were once tolerated within the church, they were condemned after the church began to insist on a singular, creedal understanding of the doctrine of the Trinity. Sixty years after its creation, the mosaic was censored as hostility toward the Arians, now defined as heretical, grew. The images of the king and his court were replaced with blank backgrounds and curtains. A hand, belonging to one of the original Arian characters, can still be seen on one of the columns.

As in this piece of art, remnants of anti-Trinitarian believers can still be uncovered, sometimes hidden just below the surface. The people of this hidden history often had ties with their monotheistic Muslim and Jewish brethren—historical connections that have been covered over as well, but can be rediscovered if we know where to look.

CONTENTS

FOREWORD

How we tell ourselves where we come from matters.

When I was growing up, my father told his children we were descendants of Theodore Parker—the brilliant, brave abolitionist, Unitarian scholar, and preacher whose ancestor Captain John Parker fired one of the first shots on Lexington Green to liberate the Colonies from British tyranny. My father was a liberal preacher himself and given his impeccable integrity as a man who lived what he professed, of course we believed his every word. My brother Ted was named after the first Theodore Parker—that sealed the deal. We children felt we were to live up to the legacy of Theodore Parker, to be heroes like him, rooted in revolutionary New England and called to assure the progress of social reform—onward and upward forever.

Turns out the real truth was something else altogether. We didn't know it until my niece Janet went sleuthing into the family history as part of a school assignment to track down her family's genealogy. She discovered that contrary to my father's story of our origins, we were not descendants of a famous New England family. In fact, we weren't even Parkers and were only very recently citizens of the U.S. Our family name was Paqua; our forebears were French immigrants who crossed the Atlantic from Normandy to the St. Lawrence seaway in the eighteenth century and settled in Canada. Somewhere along the line our name was anglicized to Parker.

When the story of our family's origins shifted, I pondered what it meant that we had believed a "cover story"—one that heightened our identity as distinguished Anglo Americans and obscured our ethnic roots in French Canada. What happens when it turns out we are not exactly who we thought we were? We find ourselves asking why realities about our identity were hidden and aspects of our history forgotten. We ponder how our understanding of who we are and what we are called to do changes with this new revelation.

Unitarian Universalists, it turns out, have an ancestry many of us have not known. Most Unitarian Universalists are familiar with the standard account of our history. We teach children about our New England roots—the pilgrims who risked everything to claim their religious freedom; the Boston reformers and literati who advanced social reform; the twentieth-century religious humanists who reverenced science, worked for civil rights, and called us to care for this world. We tell the deeper history, too, recalling our roots in Europe where sixteenth-century Unitarians in Transylvania issued the world's first "edict of religious tolerance," proclaiming that all should be free to worship by the light of their own conscience, without being coerced to conform to the dictates of the current ruling power.

There is more to the story. In this book, Susan Ritchie opens our eyes and ears to a different narrative—one that waited perhaps until this present season to come into focus. *Children of the Same God* reveals the ancestry of Unitarian Universalism at the intersections of Islam, Judaism, and Christianity in sixteenth-century Europe. Born at these intersections, Unitarians resisted establishing Christian identity over-against Muslims and Jews, and instead fostered religious views and practices that expressed kinship and mutual respect among the three traditions. This penchant for honoring relationships rather than creating divided religious identities took place among the ordinary, everyday lives of people—not only in elite circles of power.

Especially illuminating is the revelation that Unitarians are children of Islam as well as of Christianity and Judaism. I have learned from Ritchie that you can find Muslim prayer rugs in Unitarian churches in Eastern Europe. She shows how passages from the famous sixteenth-century Unitarian "Edict of Toleration" are directly traceable to Islamic texts. The fuller story this book tells is more compelling than our old story. Given the post-9/11 world in which the politics of the West rest on caricatures of Islam that are insensitive and inaccurate, the discovery of our Muslim roots now matters more than ever. The greater nuance, complexity, and grounding in truth offered by this book are important for the sake of fostering peace and understanding, at the very least.

Ritchie adds new color and depth to the vibrancy of relationships between Jews and Unitarians as well, displaying how critical this connection is to the very meaning of "Unitarian." While it is broadly understood that Unitarians opposed views of Jesus as uniquely divine and rejected doctrines of a Triune God, Ritchie shows how the debates about the Trinity cannot be narrowly understood as arguments among Christians; they mattered for relationships with Jews. She traces the story back to the proto-Unitarian perspectives debated at the fourth-century Council of Nicea, revealing how our forebears resisted the doctrinal moves that starkly and tragically separated Christians from Jews. In the sixteenth century, the Unitarian perspective gathered new import in contexts that forced violent suppression of relationships with both Muslims and Jews.

Overall, Unitarians responded to the multi-religious context of the cultures in which they lived, following a path marked by peaceful, positive, and creative interchange among Muslims, Christians, and Jews. Rather than clinging to anti-creedal rebelliousness as the hallmark of Unitarian identity, Ritchie turns our understanding toward pro-multireligious interchange as a defining characteristic of UU identity.

New vistas continue to open. This volume adds to the growing awareness that there are multiple patterns of interreligious borrowing and interchange among global religious traditions, including a variety of approaches sheltered under the banner of Unitarianism and/or Universalism in regions beyond Europe and North America. The important stories of Unitarians in the Khasi Hills of India, Unitarian Universalists in the Philippines, and new movements in Uganda and Peru add diverse examples of how Unitarian Universalists embrace kinship rather than enmity among religions. And we continue to learn that *Unitarian* has multiple meanings. A few years ago, the Moroccan minister of culture visited Starr King School for the Ministry at the invitation of Dr. Ibrahim Farajajé, Starr King's provost and professor of Islamic and Cultural Studies, who is an expert on multiple religious belongings. The minister of culture greeted our faculty with warm enthusiasm and heralded the importance of Unitarians to the culture of North Africa. In his lexicon, I was delighted to learn, *Unitarian* was synonymous with *Andalucian*—the term that refers to the nearly 700-year period in Spain and North Africa during which, under Muslim rule, Christians, Muslims, and Jews co-existed in peaceful interaction that produced a splendid flowering of the arts, architecture, music, religious interchange, and scholarship.

Surprising and delightful revelations await you in this book. As you read, ponder how this information can change present-day practices and understandings of what it means to be a Unitarian Universalist. Perhaps, for example, the popular use of the poetry of Jalal al-Din Rumi in Unitarian Universalist worship services invites us to study and consider Islam more deeply and participate more faithfully in its religious practices. Perhaps we can embrace Muslim ancestry as a meaningful part of our lineage and make a welcoming space for Muslim UUs active today. Perhaps Jewish UUs may consider their distinctive role in fostering Jewish-Muslim relationships. Perhaps even the common UU allergy to Christianity can be eased by understanding that our

Transaction # 523493
Customer # 118002

Station 3GA14

06/26/2014 12:12:37 Clerk: RYAN H

@ 12.60 9781558967250   12.60
Children of the Same God
Savings: 1.40

Subtotal   12.60
Tax @ 7.0000 %   0.88
Total   13.48
Paid: Card Mc 0589   13.48
Total Tendered   13.48
Credit (amount)   0.00

PAID BY CREDIT CARD

Card Holder   JON LUOPA
Card Number   XXXXXXXXXXXX0589
Card Type   MasterCard
Card Expires   XX/XX
Card Authorization 026687

SIGNATURE: X_____
     JON LUOPA

YOU SAVED 1.40 !!

forebears were Christians who opposed a hard, exclusivist identity for Christians.

Above all, perhaps we can be inspired to recognize a distinctive calling in our time to advocate beyond our own religious movement for multi-religious interchange and understanding—affirming kinship and relationship among religious traditions. Perhaps we can let go of fictions of purity, even about our own religious heritage, and cease our search for a unique identity. Perhaps, knowing our history better, we can more faithfully travel on the path that celebrates religious difference, religious connection, and religious "mixity" in a creative dance.

With Dr. Susan Ritchie as your guide, may your heart and mind open to the truths hidden by the old story we have told about who we are. Most especially, may you come to know something about relationships we have forgotten. May this revelation help open a new future for Unitarian Universalism in which we honor our ancestors by cultivating respect, appreciation, and justice in today's wildly pluralistic world.

—Rebecca Ann Parker

INTRODUCTION

Every culture is in itself "multicultural," not only because there has always been a previous acculturation, and because there is no pure and simple origin [provenance], but at a deeper level, because the gesture of culture is itself a mixed gesture: it is to affront, confront, transform, divert, develop, recompose, combine, rechannel.
—Jean-Luc Nancy, *Being Singular Plural*

A handful of years ago, I set out on what I was sure was a doomed mission. I was, however, hopelessly tantalized. Was there a connection between the development of Unitarianism in sixteenth-century Transylvania and the liberal Islam of the contemporary Ottoman Empire? To paraphrase Jalal al-Din Rumi (America's unlikely favorite poet) without appropriate contextualization, why not emulate Noah, and take on a project huge and foolish? I was especially curious about possible liberal Muslim influence on what has been described as Unitarianism's "most striking and distinguished" achievement in that time and place: the Edict of Torda, issued in 1568 by King John Sigismund (newly converted to Unitarianism), which the historian Earl Morse Wilbur praised as the most "perfect" principle of toleration.[1]

From our point of view today, the Edict of Torda was not exactly perfect, extending toleration to only four state-approved churches and not to other Christian and non-Christian minorities. Moreover, the edict was not equally hospitable to Catholicism and Protestantism, as is often assumed—it declared faith to be a gift from God revealed in scripture, a doctrine that is inherently Protestant.[2] Just two years prior to its issue, Sigismund had exiled Catholic priests from Transylvania. And love most likely had little to do with the edict, despite the tendency to misattribute the very modern notion that "we need not think alike to love alike" to Francis David, the edict's chief author.[3] Nonetheless, it was an impressive achievement for a young movement only beginning to coalesce. It seemed unlikely to be a mere coincidence that the edict was issued by Transylvanian Unitarians while the country was under the ultimate political rule of the religiously tolerant Ottoman Muslims. Yet historians despaired of finding direct evidence of such a connection and influence, so I set out on my quest with little hope of success.[4]

I was surprised by what I found. It was not as hard as I thought it would be to uncover the connections between Ottoman Islam and Unitarian development. Nor were the obstacles to doing so the ones that had been commonly cited: the loss of many sixteenth-century Transylvanian government documents, the resistance of the contemporary Transylvanian church to the idea of such connections, and the shortage of Unitarian historians able to access documents written in both Hungarian and Turkish.[5] All these things created their own difficulties, but I came to realize that we had overlooked evidence of influence not because of failures of information, but rather because of failures of imagination. Historical scholarship, especially church-historical scholarship, has traditionally maintained sharp borders between East and West and between Islam and Christianity. We have acknowledged that these borders may be occasionally crossed by a few spectacular individuals or ideas. Yet they are often more impenetrable in our conception than they are in the lives of actual people.

Eventually, I was able to demonstrate a direct connection between Ottoman practice and Unitarian development. Simply put, the Edict of Torda stands in direct relationship to both previous edicts and practices of toleration originating with officials of the Ottoman Empire. I present this research in chapter 2 of this book.

But as I proceeded with this work I became less interested in evidence of direct influence, and more interested in what I came to see as testimonies to the power of certain ways of living. The grounds for the religious toleration affirmed by the Edict of Torda were prepared by the everyday lives of actual people who were already living in a multi-religious way.

I became curious to know if there were other times when European Unitarianism developed through the influence of non-Christian cultures and communities, and I wanted to know the degree to which early Unitarianism might have intentionally or unintentionally embraced a willingness to cross borders.[6] European Unitarianism grew up in the soil of a variety of boundary lands in the outreaches of Eastern Europe—in Transylvania, Poland, and Lithuania. Here, far from Rome and the power centers of Luther's Germany and Calvin's Geneva, the Radical Reformation was free to take on its most progressive forms. Those declared heretics by Catholic or Protestant powers—or both—found refuge in exile. The Counter-Reformation, the Catholic Church's reclamation of souls and properties lost to Protestantism, also took longer to extend its reach to these hinterlands, allowing more time for radical ideas and communities to develop.

Unitarianism also grew up on a less literal kind of borderland, developing in the edgy shadows of a church that had long ago deemed unorthodox opinions about the nature of Jesus or the Trinity dangerously heretical. Positioned on the doctrinal border of Christianity, Unitarianism often found that its nearest theological kin were not Christian. Common causes developed and identities intermingled. As the historian Daniel Boyarin has taught us, all heretical identities—perhaps even all religions—have hybrid identities at their origins.[7]

In the end, I concluded that Unitarian identity in Europe emerged as a defense of the inherent kinship between Christianity, Islam, and Judaism. Thus Unitarianism was multicultural and multi-religious from its beginning.

Chapter 1 discusses the earliest connections between multi-religious tolerance and anti-Trinitarianism. We start at the Council of Nicea in 325, at which the rejection of Judaism becomes forever connected to the affirmation of the doctrine of the Trinity. Consequently, when later theologians (such as Michael Servetus) once again critique the Trinity, they do so partly because they also wish to reject Christian doctrines offensive to Judaism, and now also Islam. By the time Unitarian congregations gather as communities in the sixteenth century, their more radical theologians are arguing that Christianity, Islam, and Judaism have a familial relationship. These theologians specifically construed Unitarianism as a safe and conciliatory space for multi-religious relationship. Their theologies both enabled and were enabled by Unitarians' creative, real-world encounters with Muslim and Jewish communities, which I explore in chapters 2 and 3 respectively.

Chapter 4 explores a question about our contemporary North American identity which emerged in the course of this work: is it possible that, in some ways, we handled diversity and mixed identities better in our European past than we do today? While the European Unitarian tradition formed through creative engagement with Islamic and Jewish communities, the North American one did not. The precise social location of early North American Unitarianism, combined with the particular ways in which religious difference became racialized in the Americas, prevented for generations what might have otherwise been a natural multi-religious interest. However, this social location is now shifting in encouraging ways.

Perhaps reclaiming our multi-religious identity today may provide some much-needed direction for North American Unitarian Universalism. North American Unitarian Universalism has often been extraordinarily anxious about its self-image and identity. From our very inception, we have been concerned about the coherence of our movement. Predictably, these concerns tend to arise most powerfully as our congregations' demographics change. We tend to think of the generational changes within early American Unitarianism as primarily theological, but theology is never incidentally connected to culture. It is hard not to be sad and puzzled by the fact that a deliberately liberal religious tradition advocating the continuity of revelation is so often discombobulated by change. Why and how have we done such a good job of standing in our own way?

We live in interesting and promising times. More people than ever now practice, with equal vigor, both sides of a Jewish–Unitarian Universalist or Muslim–Unitarian Universalist faith. Some Muslim Unitarian Universalists have shared with me that the relationship I describe between sixteenth-century Transylvanian Unitarians and Muslims has helped them find a way in our congregations. I have also been honored to be involved in the Starr King School for the Ministry, which is intentionally and explicitly both Unitarian Universalist and multi-religious, and where I have had the honor to teach students preparing for professional religious leadership who actively identify as Muslim and Unitarian Universalist. I believe that multi-religious education is a particularly appropriate mission for a Unitarian Universalist seminary. And if, indeed, multi-religious expression is a core value for us, it is a call to reach beyond our lonely selves. Perhaps by heeding it more closely we might find a remedy for our neurosis of identity by recovering a relationship with those with whom we have shared our borderlands.

My work has taken place while many inside and outside of the academy have developed an interest in those times and places where Jews, Muslims, and Christians have lived in peaceable companionship. The late medieval (750–1492) Muslim-ruled state of al-Andalus (Arabic for Andalusia, the Iberian peninsula of present-day Spain and Portugal) is frequently invoked as a place where Jews, Muslims, and Christians managed to transform their shared conviction in the unity of God into a life of peaceful coexistence. María Rosa Menocal was one of the first to draw widespread attention to the rich multiculturalism of al-Andalus, in her 2002 *The Ornament of the World*. The phrase "ornament of the world" was coined by a German nun who never traveled to the Iberian peninsula, but who was in awe of the cultural wonders of the place as described to her by the archbishop of al-Andalus himself.

In al-Andalus, scholars from all traditions frequently could converse in all of the religious languages—Latin, Arabic, and Hebrew—and people often read each other's holy books with respect and interest. Gradually, some of the aesthetics of worship within each of the traditions took on aspects of the others. Learned and courteous debates were held. Literature, science, and the arts blossomed.

It is a clear mistake to over-romanticize Andalusia, which did have its outbreaks of hatred and violence, including the horrible anti-Semitic riots in Grenada in 1066. But even that old curmudgeon-scholar Harold Bloom has had to admit that idealization of al-Andalus is a useful beacon for our own hopes.[8]

Our deliberate Unitarian engagement with Judaism and Islam in Europe might come to serve as our own Andalusia—a remembrance and hope of what riches are possible when we embrace multi-religious engagement. Ibn al-'Arabi, the theologian who most strongly influenced the religious expression of the Ottoman Empire (as later expressed through the poetry of Jalal al-Din Rumi), described one of the realms of spiritual ascension as the imaginal. The imag-inal is a place where things are absolutely real and completely true, even though they are perceived not through the senses but through the imagination.[9] I like to think of Unitarian multi-religious engagement and enmeshment as our imaginal. Its incarnations in our movement have been variously imperfect and all too brief, but it nonetheless lies very close to the heart of our experience, and it waits, I believe, for us to overtly champion it again.

DEVELOPING HERESIES, DEVELOPING ALLIES

The Council of Nicea (c. 325) represented the first legal separation in what would ultimately become Christianity's full divorce from Judaism. The early church had permitted multiple understandings of the nature of Jesus; after Nicea, it became necessary for Christians to subscribe to a creed asserting that Jesus and God shared in the same divine substance. Never before had Christians holding to a particular theology been so clearly labeled heretics, and so severely punished for heresy: they were declared anathema, cast out of the church, and denied any possibility of salvation.

At the Council of Constantinople (c. 381), the Holy Spirit was acknowledged as the third person of the godhead, and the doctrine of the Trinity became official. Christianity was changed forever and became alienated in a new degree from its closest relatives, Judaism and paganism, as it would be in the future from Islam. As Richard Rubenstein writes in *When Jesus Became God,*

> The real thrust of [this newly defined doctrine of the Trinity] was to differentiate the Christian "Godhead," which now incorporated Jesus and the Holy Spirit, from the monolithic God worshipped by Jews, radical Arians, and, later on, by Muslims, Unitarians, Bahais and others. . . . As a result, Christians who accepted this triune God . . .

no longer shared Jehovah with their Jewish forebears or the Supreme Being with their pagan neighbors, nor could Jews or pagans claim to believe in the same God as that worshipped by the Christians.[10]

Many refused and resented this enforced separation. Jews writing in the period of the fourth-century church councils saw immediately that this shift to a fully Trinitarian Christianity would cast them dangerously outside the fold. They had good reason to be alarmed. The new theology accompanied a new and violent age of anti-Judaism.

The anti-Jewish sentiment informing the Council of Nicea was more than merely incidental to the discussion of Jesus's nature. In addition to establishing a new creed, the council also ordered Easter to be uncoupled from the Jewish religious calendar. The connection between Easter and Passover had been for years a rich source of multi-religious dialog. The elimination of that connection was one of the many signs that Christianity was trying desperately to separate itself from Judaism.[11] In a letter he sent to clergy unable to attend him at Nicea, Emperor Constantine wrote, "We ought not, therefore, to have anything in common with the Jews . . . and . . . we desire, dearest brethren, to separate ourselves from the detestable company of Jews."[12] But why did Christianity find it problematic to share God with the Jews, and eventually with the Muslims, and why did this aversion develop when it did? Discomfort with sharing God with Christians has seldom been a part of Jewish or Muslim identities.

Early Muslims, especially the Prophet Muhammad himself, were entirely convinced of the natural kinship between Judaism, Islam, and Christianity in the form of a shared God. Insistence on the unity and sameness of a God of many traditions lay at the very heart of the Prophet's revelation on Mount Hira in 610. Some Arabs practicing their indigenous religions already believed that the God, *al-Lah,* that they worshipped was the same God as that of the Jews and Christians, but Muhammad's experience transformed this belief into certain revelation.

Muhammad assumed that, like him, most Christians believed that Islam, Christianity, and Judaism were closely related, although this was partly because he underestimated the role of the Trinitarian doctrine in the Christianity of the time. Muhammad did not think that many Christians really believed that God had a son; to him, such a belief was pagan and incompatible with monotheism.[13]

In 621, Muhammad directed Muslims to fast on the Jewish high holy day of Yom Kippur, naming this fast day Asura. His mystical night journey had revealed to him the importance of Jerusalem as a holy city for Christians, Jews, and Muslims. And when the community moved to Medina, fleeing the persecutions they were encountering in Mecca, Muhammad formed this first Islamic state on the explicit notion that the many Jewish tribes, as well as pagan ones, would be "one community with the believers."[14]

The establishment of Medina brought peace between previously warring tribes. Thus, whereas ideas of tolerance in the West were theoretical, this Islamic state was, in the words of scholar Ali Kahn, "founded on the reality of actual agreement among real people of diverse ethnic and religious groups."[15] Sadly, the peace did not last. In 624, the city of Medina found itself at war with Muhammad's own tribe, the Quraysh. This accelerated the conflicts between different Muslim and Jewish tribes, and led to the expulsion of two Jewish tribes from Medina. Yet, for all the disappointment and even bloodshed, there was never any doubt on either side that Jews and Muslims were disagreeing about the wishes of the same God.

And yet, since Nicea, Christianity has insisted on the exclusivity of its God and has sometimes gone so far as to find Muslim and Jewish tolerance of Christianity objectionable. Take for one example the fascinating case of the ninth-century Christian monk Perfectus.

Perfectus was shopping in Andalusia's thriving capital city of Cordova when he was confronted by a group of Muslims who asked him if Jesus or Muhammad was the greater prophet. The question itself was most likely a trick. While tolerance was the rule of the day, to directly insult the Prophet was nonetheless a crime punishable by death. Even so, Perfectus's response to the dilemma was bizarre. Instead of finding a way around the question, he accused Muhammad of being a sexual pervert and the anti-Christ, all the while using the most terrifically obscene language. The reasonable Muslim judge who heard Perfectus's case was eager to dismiss it, given that the incident had been provoked by Muslims. But just as he was about to be set free, Perfectus, apparently unable to stop himself, issued another impossibly vulgar outburst directed at the Prophet. He was sentenced to death, upon which he became a martyr to a small band of Christians, some of whom showed up at court the very day in order to repeat the outrage.[16]

Perfectus's case is of course extreme. But it shows how some exclusivist religious identities resist a multi-religious setting even when their own tradition is tolerated. The story mirrors that of the martyrs of the early church, who often might have escaped death if they had not felt it necessary to bear defiant public witness to their faith, except for an extremely important difference: The early church martyrs lived under conditions of extreme oppression. Karen Armstrong cites the story of Perfectus early in her history of the development of a specifically Christian Islamophobia; it is one of the first moments when a particular Christian identity became not just non-Islamic, but anti-Islamic.[17]

While in the earliest days of the church Jews and Christians naturally assumed that they worshipped the same God, this comfortable sharing of a radical monotheism was eventually disrupted by Christianity's attempts to differentiate itself from Judaism by purging itself of Jewish elements. Scholars of the early church now suggest that part of the uniqueness of Christianity lies in its anxiety regarding mixed religious identities, especially Jewish and Christian. In the ninth century, this anxiety required the suppression of the history of centuries of mixed Jewish-Christian identities, together with any people, "heretics," who might still express them. As Daniel Boyarin writes, "the borders between Judaism and Christianity have been historically constructed out of acts of discursive (and too often actual) violence, especially acts of violence against the heretics who embody the instability of our constructed essences, of our terrifying bleedings into each other."[18]

This new research calls into question the traditional assumption that Christianity and Judaism "parted ways" to become distinct religions in the second century. The idea that a carefully patrolled boundary existed between Christianity and Judaism so early ignores how both traditions continued to be shaped and developed through long-lasting and considerable interchange.[19] Some scholars even suggest that it is not useful to think of Judaism and Christianity as separate "religions," because the standard understanding of a religion as a set of well-contained, homogeneous beliefs and practices is a Christian construction, and the term is meaningful only to describe Christianity, not Judaism, Islam, or other faith traditions.[20]

Insisting that Christianity separated early from Judaism makes it hard to see some of the instabilities within the heart of vernacular Christianity that are glaringly evident from another point of view. Liberal religious people who welcome multi-religious ties might recall finding an odd ally in President George W. Bush. Bush earned the ridicule of his evangelical supporters when, on a state visit to England, he remarked that he believes that Muslims and Christians are children of the same God. Learned commentators were called in, who, to many people's bemused amazement, said— in the same breath and without explaining the apparent contradiction—that Bush's belief was both representative of mainstream American Christianity and completely incompatible with the doctrine of the Trinity.[21]

But, most significantly for Unitarian history, insisting on a clear demarcation between Judaism and Christianity renders invisible those people it is our special interest to follow here—the minority who continued to identify as Christian, and yet who refused to see the rejection of multi-religious identity as a necessary or desirable expression of their faith. European Unitarianism emerged as one expression of such a liberal Christianity, intentionally honoring a close kinship with Judaism and Islam. The first step in this process took place when, by overt acts of persecution, the early church threw together Jews and Arians, inadvertently creating an interesting alliance. To see how this alliance developed, we must revisit the Council of Nicea in more detail.

I attended a non-progressive seminary, where one of the highlights of the year was the festive reenactment of the Council of Nicea by history students each spring. We reenacted these events even though we had learned only the most cartoonish version of them. The little that we knew was that around 325 Athanasius, the ambitious assistant to the bishop of Alexandria, led the greatest assembly of church leaders ever in a righteous condemnation of Bishop Arius's shocking insistence that Jesus and God were not one and the same. We were taught that Arius was a deliberately difficult and heretical person, thrilling in defiance as he left the council, refusing to sign the creed it had composed. We described only Athanasius and his co-believers as "Christian," Arius being presumably well beyond the pale. We were further told that this council cemented agreement on the divinity of Jesus for all time to come, making God's church safe from that heretical threat.

During our reenactment of the council, bands of students representing Athanasius and his followers roamed around campus carrying picket signs reading "Victory to Athanasius" and "Christianity Saved" while loudly screaming "Kill the heretic Arians." The very few of us students who were Unitarian Universalist were given the job of playing Arius and his followers. For obvious reasons, unlike the faux Athanasians, we did not throw ourselves into the role, and we did not dress in pseudo-medieval robes decorated with the name of our leader. We basically hid as much as possible, especially in the year when the celebration included carnival games where people threw darts at inflated balloons bearing the names of the characters we were playing. I was fascinated that such ancient animosities could be so easily resurrected among the ordinarily gentle and pastoral students. Only much later did I realize how terribly inaccurate this version of history was, and how it had been designed to rekindle the very hostilities we so obediently enacted.

Emperor Constantine summoned the council and held it on his lakeside property in Nicea, located in what is now Turkey. Contemporary accounts describe bishops thrilled to bask in the grandeur of the imperial palace, even if they felt little urgency to address the gathering's topic. Left to its own devices, the church might never have called this or any such conference. Fourth-century Christians were not very alarmed by the difference of opinion between Arius and the bishop of Alexandria, or anyone else for that matter, over the nature of Jesus. St. Gregory of Nyssa described the prevalence of debate regarding the divinity of Jesus:

> Every corner of Constantinople was full of their discussions: the streets, the market place, the shops of the money-changers, the victuallers. Ask a tradesman how many obols he wants for some article in his shop, and he replies with the disquisition on generated and ungenerated being. Ask the price of bread today and the baker tells you: "The son is subordinate to the father." Ask your servant if the bath is ready and he makes an answer: "The son arose out of nothing." "Great is the only Begotten," declared the Catholics, and the Arians rejoined: "But greater is He that begot."[22]

Concern about the variances of practice and belief within Christianity emerged first as Emperor Constantine's issue. A more homogenized and consolidated Christianity would make for both a better vehicle and expression of empire.

As for Arius, he was a distinguished theologian and a much-loved priest. Most bishops had fled the Roman persecution of Christianity that preceded Constantine's establishment of religious toleration in 313, but Arius refused a luxurious exile in order to stay and minister to his people. And they, especially the most oppressed among them, loved him deeply. He was especially popular among women, sailors, and dockworkers. He would teach them his theological ideas by incorporating them into lyrics for popular and even ribald tunes, which would then travel with the speed of song through the taverns and across the Mediterranean. But as gifted as Arius was, he did not develop his opinions from his own individual genius, but expressed the currents of influence shared in his church community.[23] Scholars have identified distinct Jewish influences on Arius's thinking, and even these were common among Christians of his time and place.

The very commonness of Arius's opinions meant that the issue of Jesus's divinity would not be resolved by Arius's loss at Nicea. For years, successive councils went back, forth, and sideways on the issue of Jesus's divinity, and authorities many times banished and then reinstated Arius in the established church. He was in full communion with the church when he died suddenly—during a debate, he withdrew to the toilet, where he died of an intestinal bleed. Athanasius quickly capitalized on Arius's death, concluding that God decreed his fate and that a similar doom awaited all Arians and their friends.

It is hard to say who exactly these later Arians were. The traditional teaching maintains that Arianism lingered on as a viable heresy even after the Council of Constantinople (381) authorized a radical anti-Arian persecution. According to the traditional view, after that council Arian theology survived in the semi-safe obscurity of remote Germanic areas of the empire, but even those faint traces disappeared by the seventh century at the latest. Some speculated that the persistence of anti-Arian sympathies later enabled Islam to spread rapidly in this area. This is, of course, impossible to prove; the idea may be based on comments such as those of the Byzantine emperor who, upon hearing of Muhammad for the first time, assumed he must be a kind of Arian.[24]

Yet even this mistaken linkage of Islam and Arianism suggests that we should take a closer look at what gets grouped together as "Arian" heresies. Indeed, current scholarship is no longer convinced that it makes sense even to refer to "the Arian controversy," partially because Arius may have been a minor figure, but mainly because it is clear that the rhetorical category "Arian" was invented after Arius's death for political reasons.[25] Athanasius wrote the first account of an Arian conspiracy around 339, lumping a variety of heretical views together and discrediting them by linking them to the maligned Arius. Athanasius's history not only shored up but actually invented a sense of orthodoxy in the church, even as it positioned him advantageously. Since then, much of the scholarship on the Council of Nicea has understood it as a contest between orthodox righteousness and a wickedly heretical conspiracy. But this understanding is due more to the success of Athanasius's polemics than to the actual course of events.

Interestingly for our purposes, this construction of heretical Arianism had a double effect. While it enabled multiple persecutions, it also made Arianism a category available for appropriation by later radical sects looking to connect to a history of defiance. There is no real connection between fourth-century Arian Christians and the Unitarians who emerged in the Reformation eleven centuries later. And yet the category of "Arian" remained available to those wishing to either celebrate or malign Unitarianism. In each period of Unitarian history, including the American, the enemies of the movement branded Unitarianism as the latest form of Arian infidelity. Just as often, Unitarians chose to accept the identification, fulfilling the radical Reformation desire to be connected to both a tradition of dissent and an early church not yet spoiled by complicities with empire.

But was there anything more specific about the "Ariomaniacs" (to use the slur that Athanasius made popular) that inspired and connected them to later Unitarians? After all, Ariüs's belief that Jesus was begotten (meaning that there was a time when he was not, as opposed to God, who is eternal), and that he shared in divinity but not substance with God, represents what can only be an obscure and uninteresting theological subtlety for most contemporary Unitarian Universalists.

In this and other questions about Unitarian views of the early church, it has been customary to follow the lead of the great Earl Morse Wilbur, who so generously gifted twentieth-century North American Unitarianism with its first serious appreciation of European history. Indeed, without Wilbur, American Unitarian Universalists would have precious little inkling of related movements in Europe. Working alone, Wilbur learned the necessary languages, plodded to the correct places, uncovered the right documents, and wrote thousands of pages, all the while coping with financial instability, wars, and repeated separations from his family.[26]

Yet a new generation has discovered some significant difficulties with Wilbur's method.[27] Their critiques are important, and I have rehearsed them uncomfortably for students at Starr King School for the Ministry while sitting directly under President Wilbur's large, broodingly vivid portrait. The first problem in European Unitarian history is deciding just what counts as Unitarian history when the traditions in question have little institutional continuity. Wilbur, by characterizing Unitarianism as the expression of "freedom, reason, and tolerance" in religion, cast a very large net over European history in order to catch and label as "Unitarian" whatever fish he may. Having hauled in the most interesting specimens, he then ties their stories together in such a way as to make the emergence of American Unitarianism circa 1930 (when he wrote the work) seem triumphal and inevitable. He is weak on Unitarian developments when they are very slow, when they are initially based in convictions about polity rather than theology, and when they involve entire peoples rather than remarkable individuals (as does just about the whole of our British history, and a good portion of the American). And he mentions only a few women in his whole two-volume history. All of these weaknesses impair his ability to chart or even recognize interreligious relationships and mixed identities.

For Wilbur also shared a weakness common to early twentieth-century church historians: the tendency to assume that Christian identity was solidified earlier than it was. In Wilbur's reading of our history, Arius's importance lay in demonstrating the poverty of a church that would elevate a complicated and even troubled theology to the level of unquestionable creed. But Arius could not have gone into the Council of Nicea thinking he would speak bravely against orthodoxy—orthodoxy did not yet exist.

Wilbur nonetheless asserted anti-creedal rebelliousness as the first key step in the development of "complete spiritual freedom" within what would ultimately become Unitarianism. He writes,

> First came the revolt against the bondage to the traditional dogmas as expressed in the historic Creeds, and the substitution of new statements of Christian faith drawn directly from the Scriptures. Next in logical development was . . . that if the soul were to be wholly free, reason must be accepted as the supreme authority. Nearly co-incident with this second step historically . . . came the further recognition of the equal authority of other men's reason . . . which . . . issued in the principle of full mutual tolerance of differing opinions."[28]

In this scenario, tolerance was the result of many long years of Unitarian development, not its impetus. For this reason and others, Wilbur assumed that the fourth-century church councils only influenced or prefigured later Unitarianism in minor ways, and in his histories he quickly dismisses them, writing, "The character and methods of the Councils that established these doctrines are not, it is true, calculated to give us great reverence for their

Christian character, nor much respect for their opinions."[29] Under Wilbur's influence, historians of Unitarianism still tend to assume that the Unitarian commitment to tolerance developed many centuries after the first debates regarding the doctrine of the Trinity. In doing so, they fail to see how the anti-Judaism of the council becomes mixed into the construction of heresies regarding Jesus's divinity, with the unintended consequence of creating additional common cause between anti-Trinitarians and Jews.

Athanasius famously lumped together Jews and heretical Christians, creating a mistaken, but interesting, taxonomy in which Jews and heretics became in a sense indistinguishable, at least from certain Christian vantage points. Athanasius theologized this process by contrasting the "flesh" of Judaism with the "spirit" of the new creedal Christianity.[30] He used "flesh" to characterize Judaism because he saw its embodied particularity—its very difference— as a threat to the "spirit" of a newly homogenized church. Not only did this theology inform the anti-Judaism of Nicea and later councils, it also made it possible to employ anti-Semitism against anyone resisting the imperial homogenization of the church. Soon Arians were also denounced as "flesh" in the way of "spirit." Since the Arians could not be seen as racially different, as Jews were, Athanasius portrayed them as dangerously particular by critiquing their biblical scholarship. Because they took biblical language and biblical specificity seriously, he charged, Arian scholarship, like Judaism, honored the corrupt particular over the spiritual universal. This accusation made it possible to map Arians onto existing anti-Semitic stereotypes, and the tactic rapidly became popular. Even widely celebrated hymns of the time deployed it.[31] A diverse Christendom was replaced by a monolithic Christianity and its Others, the latter now comprising both Arians and Jews.

Although spurious, the construction of Arianism fostered real sympathies between heretical Christians and their Jewish contemporaries. Jews too came to see anti-Trinitarianism, Arianism, and tolerance as connected. An early twentieth-century Jewish authority writes that, "in contrast with the domination of the orthodox church, the Arian was distinguished by a wise tolerance and a mild treatment of the population of other faiths, conduct mainly attributable to the unsophisticated sense of justice characterizing the children of nature [i.e., the Germanic peoples], but also traceable in some degree to certain points of agreement between the Arian doctrine and Judaism, points totally absent in the orthodox confession."[32]

After a long slumber, theologians in early sixteenth-century Europe, most famously Michael Servetus, once again articulated anti-Trinitarianism. This ensured that the discussion would be part and parcel of the negotiation of Jewish-Christian alliances and differences. We turn now to this part of the story.

In 1492, the European anti-Semitism that had been alarmingly growing for some three centuries culminated in the expulsion of the large Jewish community from Spain, which, as described in the introduction, had previously been the model of tolerant multiculturalism. Early that year, the last Islamic ruler of al-Andalus, Muhammad XI, was forced to hand over the Iberian peninsula to Isabella and Ferdinand of Spain in a surreal ceremony for which the Catholic nobility donned Islamic costume.[33] A few months later, Isabella and Ferdinand issued the order expelling anyone maintaining a Jewish identity. Approximately half a million Spanish Jews left for the safety of the Islamic-ruled Middle East, while an equal number declared their conversion to Christianity and remained in their native land. Some of these "conversos" understandably attempted to continue to practice their religion in secret. The Spanish Inquisition originally targeted these "Marranos" or "crypto-Jews."

Muslims were given the same choice between exile and conversion, although slightly later and at different times in the different polities that made up Spain. The edict went out in 1502 in Castile and in 1526 in Aragon. In Valencia, where perhaps a third of the population consisted of Muslims protected by the nobles, who benefited from their inexpensive labor, authorities withdrew tolerance more slowly. They forcibly baptized many Muslims, and thus considered those Muslims to have converted, during the Germania rebellions of 1521–22. Not surprisingly, many of these Moriscos, as they came to be called, continued to practice their faith in a variety of private ways in the following years. In 1525 authorities told Muslims in Valencia to convert or face exile, although they granted them a forty-year assimilation period before turning over to the Inquisition those still practicing Islam. The regime required the Muslims to choose between exile and conversion a final time in 1609.[34] As the practice of the faith withdrew behind closed doors, becoming a part of private domestic life, Muslim women took on more important roles in its maintenance, encouraging spiritual practice and quietly teaching the next generation essential traditions.[35] Some women regularly hid sacred texts on their bodies to protect them from seizure.[36] In doing so, they assumed great risk, as the Inquisition felt little obligation to respect the traditional privacy of the Muslim household or the modesty of Muslim women.

Some Jewish "New Christians" navigated these dangerous waters by accepting Christianity but deliberately not engaging with the more divisive and doctrinal aspects of the faith. One such was Juan de Valdes (1509–41), who helped to define a Christian humanism, with an inspirational focus on everyday spirituality, self-examination, and love. Other New Christians wrestled more overtly with the doctrines that were the most offensive from a Jewish point of view, the chief of which proved to be, not surprisingly, that of the Trinity. Pedro Gonzalez, tried by the Inquisition in 1525, described his opposition to Christian conversion this way: "The old and new laws are very similar, for if the Jews believed in the Trinity, the creeds would be the same."[37]

The Spanish authorities hoped to resolve their anxieties about multi-religious living by establishing a homogeneous Christian state. But instead of guaranteeing a monolithic Christian adherence, outlawing Judaism and Islam raised the threat of mixed and cloaked Jewish-Christian and Muslim-Christian identities, thus raising anxiety to new and violent heights. The Inquisition aimed to ferret out people with inauthentic Christian identities, but even its widespread terrors could not guarantee religious purity. Indeed, the practice of forced conversion made it impossible to determine which conversions were "authentic."

Hence Spain began to enact laws of *limpieza de sangre,* purity of blood. These stated that Christian identity could be guaranteed only by a direct bloodline connection to families who had been Christian for many generations. These laws radically conflated religious and racial identity. Historians suggest that this obsessive linkage of racial purity and religion gave birth to modern anti-Semitism (prejudice against Jews on account of their racial identity, as distinguished from anti-Judaism, which is based on religious identity). Some go further, arguing that the purity of blood laws are the root of all modern racisms.[38]

Michael Servetus, the most famous anti-Trinitarian of the day and the chief inspiration for most of the founders of institutional Unitarianism, was a part of this cultural context. He was not a New Christian, but he so deeply understood that point of view that one of his biographers wonders if "Servetus was not in reality presenting some Christian understanding of Judaism based on a complete course in Jewish converso politics."[39] He was familiar with the Jewish commentators both of the early Christian era and of his own time, and with their arguments against the Trinity. He was also well read in the radical attacks on the Trinity coming from the exiled Jews living under the protection of the Ottoman Empire. In other words, although Servetus was not actually a New Christian, he was well enculturated as one. The historian Richard Popkin has even argued, not without controversy, that the connection between Jewish influence and anti-Trinitarianism is so strong that the category of "Marrano" might justly extend to cover not only those who maintained their Jewish faith in secret, but all those who refused to fully embrace the doctrine of the Trinity, regardless of their background.[40]

Part of Servetus's motivation for taking on the Trinity was his concern that the doctrine unnecessarily separates Christianity from Judaism and Islam. In *The Errors of the Trinity*, he praises Islam's acceptance of Jesus as a prophet and regrets that Christianity does not return the favor by acknowledging Muhammad. He expresses concern that the doctrine of the Trinity, especially in some of the extreme articulations of the time, made a laughingstock of Christianity. And he describes medieval Biblical commentator Rabbi Kimhi's criticisms of the Trinity, which, he weeps to say, Christian theologians never fully responded to.[41]

While jokes of the time about the difficulty of finding true Trinitarians in Spain suggest that many people shared Servetus's point of view, the expanding focus of the Inquisition soon forced vocal dissenters from the country. Many brilliant and independent thinkers, including Servetus, ranged across Europe in search of toleration, and Servetus's post-exile career is the most fabulous among the many fabulous stories that emerged from this ferment. Moving to France, he worked under an assumed name as an editor and then as a physician (with the local archbishop chief among his supporters and patients). He could not, however, stop himself from theologizing, publishing his work, and even sending it on to John Calvin, who was no more fond of him than the Inquisition had been. So it was that John Calvin had him executed in Geneva in 1553.

The next generation of anti-Trinitarians, most notably Niccolo Paruta, Jacob Paleologus, Szymon Budny, and Giorgio Biandrata, provides the link between Servetus's theology and the purposeful establishment of Unitarian churches. For in Poland, Transylvania, and Lithuania, these men deliberately gathered religious communities around anti-Trinitarian ideas inspired by Servetus.[42] While Budny's and Paleologus's theology often stands out as more radical than that of the gathered Unitarian churches, their thinking helped found European Unitarianism.

Jacob Paleologus (c. 1520–85) provided the most comprehensive articulation within early Unitarianism of a natural kinship between Christianity, Judaism, and Islam. He was a Dominican monk born in Greece; he probably took the name Paleologus to imply a connection with the Byzantine royal family. He took refuge in Prague in 1559 when a theological paper he wrote on revelation attracted the interest of the Inquisition. There he lived as a scholar of the Middle East and of the Quran, and there too he began identifying as a Unitarian, entering into a correspondence with Francis David, the leader of what would become the Transylvanian Unitarian church. Eventually he accepted David's invitation to serve as rector of the Unitarian school in Kolosvar. He is primarily remembered in Unitarian history for urging the Polish church to abandon its pacifist conviction, concerned that if people of faith refused to take arms, enemies of justice might easily take power. Unfortunately, little attention has been paid to his conception of the role that Unitarianism might play in bringing Christianity, Judaism, and Islam together as a single religious family.

One of Paleologus's more extraordinary works is his *Disputatio scholastica*, written in 1570. It depicts an imaginary church council, which includes not only representatives of the different Christian confessions, but also Jews and Muslims. In a fantasy that must have given Paleologus great satisfaction, Pope Pius (who was Grand Inquisitor during Paleologus's own persecution) is summoned from the deepest level of hell and made to admit that he exercised his authority ruthlessly and unfairly and that he seriously misunderstood scripture.

But at the heart of the council is a debate between Trinitarians and anti-Trinitarians. Heavenly elders, including Jesus himself, have asked God to intervene to prevent what they see as excessive and even cruel attempts to foist Jesus's divinity on the church. Defending the anti-Trinitarian point of view are Niccolo Paruta (a famed Italian anti-Trinitarian) and Johann Sommer (Francis David's son-in-law). Representing the Trinitarian argument are Theodore Beza (John Calvin's successor) and other popes summoned from hell for the purpose: Gregory VII and Boniface VIII. Somewhat unfairly, the debate is presided over by the Transylvanian Unitarian king John Sigismund. Not surprisingly, the anti-Trinitarians win the argument.

The piece is notable for its curious yet rich literary style. Paleologus seems to have special fun discussing the lavish setting: half heavenly Jerusalem, half parody of a papal or imperial residence. But the work has prompted scholars of the sixteenth century to reexamine the motivations behind early anti-Trinitarianism. Peter Schaeffer writes, "Other early dissenters had not so much rejected a belief in the Trinity as the codification of this belief in abstract unscriptural terminology such as substance, essence, hypostasis and relation, and its ruthless imposition by persecution and terror, yet here the Trinity is rejected as the emblem of tyranny and intolerance, whether seated in Rome, Wittenberg, Geneva, or anywhere else."[43]

In condemning intolerance, was Paleologus condemning only Christianity's intolerance of theological diversity, or was he condemning something larger? His *De tribus gentibus*, published together with the *Disputatio,* suggested a radical basis for understanding Jews, Muslims, and Christians as members of the same religious family.

The heart of Paleologus's vision is simple. Jews, Christians, and Muslims are all a part of the same Semitic family tree, and all understand salvation to involve seeing Jesus's teachings as prophetic. The details are rather confusing, because he did not always fully understand the traditions he was so anxious to join together (the case of Jews who accept Jesus as a teacher but not as the Messiah gets him into some especially murky and troublesome water). He even argues at one point that Muslims are not just theological but genetic Christians: since Islam has become prevalent in some formerly Christian areas, the races must have mixed. But he works hard to establish a genetic family history, because his vision of true kinship is so strong and, most importantly, based on actual experience.

In 1573 Paleologus traveled to Constantinople, where he was impressed by Ottoman religious toleration. His own account of his travels is possibly inaccurate and certainly grandiose; he claimed to have made contact with many impressive officials of the Ottoman Empire, some of whom were likely dead by the time of his journey. And yet his story opens up an exciting chapter in early Unitarian history, in which the theologies of multi-religious toleration sometimes promote creative cultural exchanges with contemporary Jewish and Islamic communities, and in which the experience of living in multi-religious, multicultural communities sometimes gives rise to tolerant theologies.

The world's religions and cultures have been more enmeshed in creative conflict, mutual attraction, and reciprocal influence than scholarship has fully imagined. We have yet to assemble the full puzzle, of course, but as we do so, we must take care that the histories we produce of different ethnicities, religions, and cultures acknowledge that the boundaries between them have been continually negotiated and crossed. And we shall want to pay special attention to those, such as the early European Unitarians, who made their home in the borderlands.

In the next chapter I will explore the patterns of mutual influence among these communities by examining the basis for the Edict of Torda, which granted religious toleration. It derived not just from Francis David's own ideas or from European humanist influence, nor was it solely due to the direct political and legal influence of the Ottoman Empire. Rather, it was rooted in the everyday lives of actual people, who were already living in multi-religious and multicultural ways.

TWO

EUROPEAN UNITARIANISM AND OTTOMAN ISLAM

John Sigismund, the son of John Zapolya, king of Hungary and *voivode* (governor) of Transylvania, was born in July 1540. Sultan Suleyman of the Ottoman Empire considered the birth so important that he sent a representative to stand in a corner of Queen Isabella's room to watch over her and the infant.[44] John Zapolya died just two weeks after his son's birth, and on his deathbed he instructed that his son be named heir to his titles, violating a previous agreement that promised Hungary after his death to Ferdinand, the brother of the Hapsburg Emperor Charles. When it became clear after John's death that his successors had no intention of allowing Hungary to become a part of the Hapsburg Empire, Ferdinand responded by laying siege to the Hungarian capital, Buda. In 1541, with Queen Isabella's forces nearing collapse, Sultan Suleyman appeared in Buda with a large army, successfully repulsing Ferdinand and establishing a lasting strategic partnership with Isabella. Suleyman claimed direct control of Buda and much of lower Hungary, allowing Isabella and her infant son to rule Transylvania under his authority.

After some years of political contrivance and redefinition, Transylvania developed a new identity as a border state, a semi-independent buffer between areas directly controlled by the Hapsburgs and the Ottomans. It also became one of the safest places in Europe for the development of progressive Protestantism. In 1568, the now grown-up King John Sigismund, newly converted to Unitarianism, issued the Edict of Torda, which historians have celebrated as the first European policy of expansive religious toleration.[45] It says,

> His majesty, our Lord, in what manner he—together with his realm—legislated in the matter of religion at the previous Diets, in the same matter now, in this Diet, reaffirms that in every place the preachers shall preach and explain the Gospel each according to his understanding of it, and if the congregation like it, well. If not, no one shall compel them for their souls would not be satisfied, but they shall be permitted to keep a preacher whose teaching they approve. Therefore none of the superintendents or others shall abuse the preachers, no one shall be reviled for his religion by anyone, according to the previous statutes, and it is not permitted that anyone should threaten anyone else by imprisonment or by removal from his post for his teaching. For faith is the gift of God and this comes from hearing, which hearing is by the word of God.[46]

Rather than establishing his own faith as the national religion and compelling his people to adopt it, as was the custom of rulers, Sigismund made it legal for them to practice their own traditions. Moreover, he allowed congregations to choose their own preachers, preventing church and state authorities from manipulating religious choice by forcing unpopular theology on people, and he supported the right of preachers to teach their own understandings of the Gospel.

The story of the Edict of Torda's proclamation of religious toleration can be understood as a shared Islamic-Unitarian undertaking, the result of reciprocal influence and creative exchange between two cultures sharing close contact and mutual respect.

This is not a story about Ottoman history with a few footnotes about Unitarians, nor a story about Unitarian history with a few footnotes about the Ottomans. Rather, it is the story of a place where these two cultures creatively mixed and mingled.

Traditional accounts hold that the brilliant Unitarian court preacher Francis David was singularly responsible for inspiring King Sigismund to issue the Edict of Torda. Many Unitarian Universalist churches have prints of Aladár Körösfoi-Kriesch's 1896 painting depicting King Sigismund, his court, representatives from the different religious traditions, and the nobility all listening intently as David argues for toleration. While David speaks, with arms upstretched, a single ray of sunlight shines directly on his head. The painting clearly implies that God is directly implanting the principle of toleration in David's brain so that he may bring it into the world, complete and whole. I call this the "immaculate conception" theory of the edict, in that it ignores the many influences on the edict's development and the many cultural conditions that had to exist for toleration to become thinkable.

To begin with, the influence of Giorgio Biandrata (1515–88), John Sigismund's court physician, on David, and indeed on the development of Unitarianism in general, cannot be overestimated. Biandrata does appear in Körösfoi-Kriesch's painting, silently looking on from the sidelines as David holds forth, but he is a more fascinating and dynamic figure than this positioning might suggest. He had been inspired by the anti-Trinitarian thinking of Michael Servetus while living in Poland, and he brought this influence to the Transylvanian court along with the rich traditions of Italian humanism. David's own anti-Trinitarian leanings developed partially through conversations with Biandrata. And, perhaps more than anyone else, Biandrata was interested in coalescing anti-Trinitarian theologies into an intentional Unitarian church.

The esteemed historian of the Hungarian-speaking people of Transylvania, Mihály Balázs, has cautiously proposed that the French reformist Sebastian Castellio may also have influenced

David's understanding of tolerance. Castellio was horrified at Servetus's execution for heresy, famously remarking that "to kill a man is not to protect a doctrine, but it is to kill a man."[47] It is logical to think of Castellio in connection with the development of tolerance, although Balázs notes that his theology subtly differs from David's and there is no evidence that David had access to Castellio's mature works.[48]

Those with a thoughtful regard for feminism have further expanded the number of influences on the Edict of Torda by restoring Queen Isabella to the story. A dedicated humanist, Isabella had been a member of the learned and liberal Polish royal court. She insisted that her son learn the values of classical humanism. Some authorities even claim her as the originator of toleration in Transylvania, noting that, as regent for her underage son, she issued an edict of toleration herself in 1557. This is an exaggeration, as Isabella's edict did not establish religious toleration, but rather asked the warring Catholics and Lutherans to refrain from violence.[49] Clearly, though, many historians understand that the Edict of Torda derived not just from David's personal genius, but also from liberal cultural influences.

And yet, with the exception of Alicia Forsey's study of the relationship between Isabella and Suleyman, there are no narratives of non-European and non-Christian influences on the edict. On investigation, however, it becomes clear that these narratives have been erased. Hungarian church historians and the Hungarian Unitarian Church vehemently deny any Ottoman influence on the development of Unitarianism. Turkey is a historic enemy of the Hungarian nation, and Hungarians, understandably, associate the Ottomans with violence and oppression. Hence, some of the most nationalistic Hungarian historians even reject what has long been accepted elsewhere: that Protestant movements such as Unitarianism would never have developed and matured in Hungary and Transylvania as much as they did if the Ottoman Empire's political protection of the region had not delayed the arrival of the Counter-Reformation.[50]

Histories written outside Hungary are more likely to acknowledge Ottoman influence, but still often in very limited ways. George Huntson Williams's famous work *The Radical Reformation* is an example. Williams acknowledges in a footnote that Ottoman religious tolerance may have influenced the development of Unitarianism in Transylvania, yet he understands this influence as exclusively political, negative, and unidirectional. He suggests that the Ottomans cynically promoted tolerance in order to inflame local divisions and thus enhance their own political control.[51] This is of course partially true; Ottoman domination succeeded in part because of their flexibility and acceptance of local customs. And yet there is more to the story: The policy of tolerance was more than a matter of military strategy, and it found its expression not only in political structures but also in everyday life.

As the Ottoman scholar Victoria Holbrook reminds us, "The Ottomans are perhaps most unique for including and synthesizing the cultural elements of the land through which they passed. They are known for creating structures by which the people who had lived there before could carry on their lives and their beliefs in the way that they chose."[52] The Ottomans permitted a variety of religious and cultural expressions for reasons of bureaucratic expedience in their expanding empire, but toleration was also deeply rooted in their own legal, cultural, and religious traditions.

Any monotheist willing to accept the political rule of the Ottomans was given protection and legal rights by the empire. The Ottomans generally observed the established Islamic tradition with respect to religious minorities, the *dhimma* or "protected persons." Non-Muslims paid a special tax, and in return the state treated them as it did its Muslim subjects. The Ottomans also placed some mild restrictions on religious minorities, to mark them as socially inferior to Muslims. However, these restrictions were widely ignored.[53]

The sultan had particular reasons to promote tolerance. He benefitted from protecting travelers who might convey information and goods from one part of the empire to the other, so long as they maintained allegiance to him. And such travelers might well belong to religious minorities.[54]

Toleration, then, derived from Ottoman policy, Ottoman bureaucratic structure, and Ottoman interpretation of Islam, which was in most instances stunningly liberal, cosmopolitan, and pluralistic. As anti-Semitism increased elsewhere in Europe, Jews found the Ottoman Empire an enormously hospitable place, and a learned diasporic community grew and thrived within its borders. For this reason, Salo Baron described the sixteenth century as one of Judaism's great golden ages.[55] Christians, as another "people of the book," enjoyed a similar welcome in Ottoman society, especially those fleeing persecution by other Christians.[56] Ottoman flexibility had other advantages for religious radicals. We know, for example, that Unitarians published some of their more radical literature in Turkey and had it smuggled into Transylvania.[57]

With the Ottoman dimension of the story so obvious, why has there been such resistance to it, such anxiety about the possibility of Eastern influence? We must bear in mind the lingering effects of Hungarian nationalism. One of the political results of the Reformation was a certain identification of Hungarian patriotism with liberal Protestantism, and Hungarian nationalists sometimes represent Unitarianism as a national religion, sprung fresh and whole from Hungarian soil and uniquely suited to the spirit of the Hungarian people.[58] Crediting the historical enemy with having inspired Unitarianism is theologically, ethnically, and politically threatening. Indeed, some of those who have dared to suggest a connection between Islam and Unitarianism have done so precisely in order to discredit Unitarianism as un-Hungarian. Alexander Sándor Unghváry's *The Hungarian Protestant Reformation in the Sixteenth Century under the Ottoman Impact* provides an especially remarkable example of this. In an attempt to dismiss Unitarianism as a form of Islam (and therefore dismiss it as un-Hungarian), Unghváry suggests that David was more Islamic than Christian. He claims Servetus as David's greatest influence, and then suggests that Servetus's anti-Trinitarianism was not a form of Christianity but of pure Islam. He claims that Servetus quoted Muhammad with more relish and frequency than the Bible.[59] Oddly, he cites as his source for Servetus's reliance on the Quran a page of Earl Morse Wilbur's work that in fact praises Servetus's familiarity with and sophisticated use of the Bible, making no mention of the Quran. It's certainly true that Servetus knew a great deal about Islam and Judaism, as well as Christianity, and that he wanted them to remain in close relationship. The fact that Unghváry was both so wrong and so right suggests that it might be more fruitful to look for evidence of Islamic influence on Unitarianism in anti-Unitarian propaganda than in more sympathetic histories.

Indeed, the only literature that has documented an Ottoman Islamic influence on Transylvanian Unitarianism is that of the anti-Unitarian movements of seventeenth- and eighteenth-century Europe. The eighteenth-century French historian Maturin Veyssière de La Croze, for example, explicitly connected Islamic theology, the Quran, and the development of Unitarianism in Transylvania, claiming that Transylvanian Unitarians themselves saw their non-Trinitarian theology as corresponding exactly with the Quranic unity of God.[60] Writers such as La Croze were generally convinced—and alarmed—that Unitarianism might be a step toward conversion to Islam. This belief dates to the earliest days of Protestantism, when Catholics and Protestants alike (including Martin Luther himself) saw the spread of Islam as both an extension of anti-Trinitarian heresies and a consequence of divine wrath. From this perspective, Islam was both just a new form of Unitarianism and a divine punishment on Christendom for not eradicating Unitarianism. Martin Luther himself believed this, and the notion stuck because it appealed to people seriously worried about Islam in both a religious and a political way. Ironically, at the same time Luther, Phillip Melanchthon, and other leading Protestants repeatedly praised Turkish tolerance, contrasting it with papal oppression.[61]

It is easy for us to forget how frightened Europeans were that the Ottoman Empire might one day dominate Western Europe. They had good reason to fear; at the height of their power, the Ottomans were knocking on the gates of Vienna. Europeans were also, justifiably, concerned that the Unitarians' cultural and theological interest in Islam might lead them to make political alliances with the Ottoman Empire. Cultural exchange is not viewed positively in times of change and fear. But the fear prevalent in Europe at that time gave birth to many of the forms of Islamophobia that still plague us today.[62]

Adam Neuser was one Unitarian whose theology not only drew him toward Islam but led him to actually propose an alliance with the Ottomans. He wrote to Sultan Suleyman suggesting that well-born, educated, anti-Trinitarian Christians might bring much of Europe over to the Ottomans, if Suleyman were to invite them to ally with him. His letter was intercepted and Neuser was imprisoned, but he eventually escaped, moved to Turkey, and embraced Islam. Similarly, in 1682 London Unitarians planned to approach the Moroccan ambassador, Mohammad ben Hadou, with a letter proposing a Unitarian-Ottoman alliance. While this letter was largely respectful of Islam, it insensitively suggested ways Islam could be improved with Unitarian guidance, proposing that remnant "repugnancies" (contradictions) in the Quran would pose no problem to Muslims if they would only begin to read scripture in a historical and critical way, just as the Unitarians had come to read the Bible.[63] This was, of course, highly offensive, since scriptural infallibility is central to Islam. The letter seems never to have been delivered, but it is interesting that its memory was preserved not by the Unitarians but by the active anti-Unitarian C. Leslie. He used it as evidence of the political untrustworthiness of Unitarians.

And so, as we return to Transylvania, we know to look for traces of Ottoman-Unitarian interaction not in the standard histories, but in anti-Islamic and anti-Unitarian propaganda.

The most widespread and popular form of anti-Islamic propaganda in Hungary at the time of the Edict of Torda consisted of lurid accounts of alleged Turkish atrocities. Hapsburg imperial officials, keen on inflaming ethnic hatred of the Turks, aimed their materials at the liberal Protestants living under significant religious oppression in the lands bordering Hungary, lest they be tempted to see the tolerant Ottomans as friends.[64] Indeed, interesting new work on the European literature of the time shows that Europeans deliberately constructed the stereotype of Muslim women as oppressed in order to offend liberal Christians who might otherwise have been attracted to Islam.[65] In general, much of the ideological literature of this time and place set out to deny that Turks and Hungarians influenced each other at all. But they did, and, as is so often the case, the denial of these mutual influences only betrays considerable anxiety over their extent.

For instance, one story tells of a Lutheran minister who, while entertaining Turkish guests for dinner, is tricked into replacing his hat with a turban. His guests announce that donning the turban constitutes converting to Islam, and they follow up this forcible conversion with a forcible circumcision. This dinner-table operation is all the more hideous, the text informs us, because it supposedly excludes the man forever from Christian ministry. It is not difficult to read such stories as originating from a fear that ethnic identity will be lost through conversion, assimilation, and the increasing cultural enmeshment of the Other, especially when the stories focus, as they often do, on the "execrable Turkish custom of seducing Christian women."[66] Surprisingly, these stories still appear in modern Hungarian histories, usually cited as evidence against the claim that Ottoman rule promoted the development of Protestantism.[67] But the irony is that, in their eagerness to prove Muslim religious intolerance and beastly behavior, these accounts actually preserve evidence of considerable cultural enmeshment: Turkish guests at European dinners, Lutheran clergy converting to Islam, Turks and Hungarians marrying and having children together, and Europeans relocating to the heart of the Ottoman Empire.[68]

There is considerable evidence of intermarriage in sixteenth- and seventeenth-century Hungary, both between Turks and Hungarians and between members of different religious confessions. Early sixteenth-century Hungarian Reformed canon law devotes enough energy to prohibiting marriage between Muslims and Christians to indicate the prevalence of such marriages. And intermarriage between members of the different Christian churches of Transylvania seems to have been common even before the Edict of Torda was proclaimed. It was commonly understood that sons would follow the tradition of their father and daughters that of their mother. For example, the early seventeenth-century historian Kozma Petrityvity described the rather complicated religious mix of his family as not unusual. His grandfather was Unitarian, his grandmother Catholic; his mother was raised Catholic, although one of her siblings became Reformed. She married a Unitarian, who raised his sons (including Petrityvity) to be Unitarians, even as the daughters attended mass with their mother.[69]

Consider as well stories of the supposed forced relocation of Christian Europeans by the Ottomans. Just as with the stories of forced conversions and marriages, there is evidence of mutual influence where we have been asked to see only unidirectional oppression.

Niyazi Berkes, in his excellent study of Turkish secularism, discusses the case of Ibrahim Müteferrika. Eighteenth-century European sources describe him as a young Hungarian Calvinist studying for the ministry who was captured and enslaved by the Turks in the early 1690s, condemned to a life of misery in Ottoman lands. He eventually converted to Islam, only in order to escape slavery. Now we know that Ibrahim was in fact a Unitarian raised in Kolosvar, a man whose anti-Trinitarian convictions genuinely drew him toward Islam. He also thrived rather than suffered in the heart of the Ottoman Empire, eventually establishing the first modern printing press in a Muslim land. His treatise "Risale-I Islamiye," published on his own press in 1710, was dismissed by eighteenth-century historians as a pro-Islamic tract, but it is far more complicated—and more Unitarian—than that. According to Berkes, not only is "Risale-I Islamiye" clearly the work of an anti-Trinitarian Christian, it also indicates that Ibrahim was attracted to Islam before he left Transylvania. Berkes concludes, "If we go back one century and trace the development of religious and political conditions in Transylvania, we shall not fail to appreciate that neither Transylvanian Unitarianism nor Ibrahim's folk were unfamiliar with or too distant from Islam."[70]

Contemporary literature also tells the story of Péter Pérenyi, a sixteenth-century Protestant Hungarian noble who "left his young son, Ferenc, in Turkish hands as a hostage, only himself to endure detention some years later."[71] Upon further investigation, Pérenyi proves to have been an unorthodox Christian neither unfamiliar with nor distant from Islam, a minor noble who sought refuge with the Ottomans when his neighbors targeted him because of his advocacy of religious toleration.

The Turks did sometimes enslave Eastern European Christian boys, in what was called the *devshirme*, or "collection." (Because they were subjects of the Ottoman Empire, their enslavement was technically illegal, since Christians were supposed to have the same rights as Muslims.[72]) Although this fate sounds horrible, the boys chosen for imperial service received what many describe as the best care and education available anywhere in the world at that time. Many Turkish parents even attempted to disguise themselves as Christians so that their children might be afforded this honor.[73] These boys often grew up to hold powerful administrative positions, and they did much to ease relations between the empire and their hometowns.[74] Indeed, the Ottomans deliberately groomed Europeans for positions of power, finding it safer to place Europeans in the empire's highest posts than Turks who might belong to families with dynastic claims rivaling those of the Ottomans.

Given that the Hungarian Unitarian boys often did better in their Islamic education than others taken in the *devshirme,* it is tempting to speculate about the presence of these Hungarian Muslim-Unitarians in the highest of Ottoman places. We know that eleven of the twenty-one grand viziers most credited with Ottoman success (those who directed the imperial administration between 1453 and 1623) were South Slavs. Most of the viziers after 1521 came from the Western part of the Balkans.[75] And hence I am not embarrassed to extend our rather dubious tradition of claiming illustrious ancestors by suggesting that some of the grand viziers of the Ottoman Empire may have been Unitarians.

We can see, then, that the Edict of Torda was promulgated in a context of more intercultural enmeshment than we might have expected. Knowing this, let us return to tell again the tale of the edict, beginning with events two decades prior to its issuance.

On August 24, 1548, the Catholic authorities in Tolna asked the sultan's representative in Buda to take action against the Hungarian Protestant pastor in their city, Imre Szigeti. Offended by Pastor Szigeti's unapologetic and public advocacy of reformed ideas, they wanted him either killed or driven from the city. The chief intendant of the pasha of Buda told them, however, that not only had the pasha denied their request, he had also issued an edict of toleration stating, in part, that "preachers of the faith invented by Luther should be allowed to preach the Gospel everywhere to everybody, whoever wants to hear, freely and without fear, and that all Hungarians and Slavs (who indeed wish to do so) should be able to listen to and receive the word of God without any danger. Because—he said—this is the true Christian faith and religion."[76]

The pasha's edict is not mentioned in any of the Unitarian histories. (In fairness, many of the records and accounts of the Ottoman governors of Buda have been lost or destroyed, although their reputation for establishing equitable relations between Christendom and Islam lives on even in the Hungarian chronicles.[77])

And yet it has much in common with the edicts of toleration that would emerge from John Sigismund's court. The 1568 Edict of Torda argues against compulsion in religion, "for faith is the gift of God and this comes from hearing, which hearing is by the word of God." This wording is taken from Romans 10:17: "so then faith comes by hearing, and hearing by the word of God." And while the pasha's 1548 edict doesn't echo scripture as closely as the 1568 one, it similarly states that faith is that which is received from God through free adherence to his word. This assertion is hardly unique, of course: it's an expansion of the basic Protestant principle. But it is interesting that the Edict of Torda should employ it.

And while no direct evidence exists that Francis David knew of the pasha's 1548 edict when he laid the groundwork for the Edict of Torda two decades later, it is hard to imagine that he did not. Like David, Imre Szigeti had been a Hungarian student at Wittenberg, and indeed, we know of the pasha's edict through a letter from Szigeti to a former classmate in Germany, Matthias Flacius, whom David also knew. (Flacius published the letter in Germany in 1550 in order to dramatize the contrast between Catholic oppression of Protestants and Islamic tolerance.[78]) In 1548, while Szigeti was serving the Lutheran church in Tolna, David was serving one in Bistrita (Beszterce), placing him closer to Buda than Szigeti. The Magyar Lutherans elected David as their superintendent in 1557, and it would have been the pasha's edict establishing toleration of the churches that he administered.

Moreover, the pasha's action corresponds with other, better recorded events. We know, for example, that in 1574 in Lower Hungary, two preachers championing the Unitarian cause were persecuted for heresy by local authorities under outdated, pre-toleration laws. Lukas Tolnai managed to escape, but George Alvinczi was put to death by order of a church court presided over by a Calvinist bishop. Influential Unitarians knew to turn to the pasha at Buda for assistance. Eager to assist them, the pasha declared the execution of Alvinczi "inhumane" and ordered the

CHILDREN OF THE SAME GOD

bishop and his two fellow judges to be killed. Only when the Unitarian preacher at Pécs interceded, saying that Unitarians did not want such drastic revenge, did the pasha remit the sentence, imposing in lieu of it a heavy annual tribute on the entire locale.[79] And we know that historians have underestimated the influence of the Ottoman legal system on the development of the Reformation. During the 1550s, 1560s, and 1570s, Protestants in Hungarian lands directly ruled by the Ottomans arranged for their doctrinal debates with the Catholics to be presided over by Turkish officials, who assured Protestant triumphs by either direct ruling or indirect tampering. Turkish officials were similarly the ultimate authority behind Protestant edicts issued in the wake of such debates.[80] It was also commonplace for non-Muslims to bring legal cases to Muslim courts, which were commonly understood to be more liberal than those of other denominations.[81]

But let us leave the story of direct influence there, for it would not do for this to distract from the emerging portrait of two cultures more enmeshed in creative engagement, mutual attraction, and reciprocal influence than we have imagined before. There are, of course, many pieces of the portrait yet to be assembled, but let us assemble them not in an effort to tell an ethnically distinct cultural history, but with an eye to the many ways in which the borders between the Ottoman and Hungarian cultures were in this period crossed, recrossed, and renegotiated. The basis for the Edict of Torda was established not only by Francis David and the other powerful men who articulated it, nor through European humanist influence, nor even through the direct political and legal influence of the Ottoman Empire. The grounds for religious toleration were prepared by the people who intermarried before their leaders proclaimed toleration and who were attracted to Islam and understood the protection it offered to progressive Protestants.

Could it be that toleration, that most precious gift of the European Enlightenment, was instead a shared liberal Christian-Muslim undertaking? Ironically, while we praise the earliest Uni-

34

tarian statements of religious toleration as progressive promotions of diversity, we also firmly define them as products of liberal European genius. It is well past time to live out the paradigm of mutual influence that we have already heralded.

THREE

EUROPEAN UNITARIANISM AND JUDAISM

As we have seen, European Unitarianism was shaped in large part by the desire to honor Christianity's close kinship with Judaism and Islam. Convinced that Christians, Muslims, and Jews were a part of the same religious family, Unitarians resisted theologies of God that could not be freely shared across these traditions. Eventually, their theology spurred them to establish actual relationships with their Jewish and Islamic kin. This chapter examines the connections early European Unitarians made with contemporary Jewish communities. It reveals not only the promise, but the perils of those border crossings.

The heart of the matter can be located at the intersection of two stories. One story is about the loss of a friendship. Between 1575 and 1581, something happened to alienate the Unitarian leader Martin Czechowic of Lublin, Poland, and a rabbi named Jacob who lived in the small town of Belzyce not far away. The two men had been quite close, and their faith communities had supported them in their friendship. Yet, by the end of the sixteenth century, a relationship such as theirs had become inconceivable.

The other story is about how, in the twentieth century, the eastern Transylvanian village of Bozodujfala was destroyed, closing a special chapter in the history of Unitarian multi-religious engagement. This four-hundred-year-old village, while small, was remarkably religiously diverse, with congregations of Catholics, Reformed Christians, Unitarians, and Jews, including Szekely Jews. Szekely Jews were originally Unitarians who adopted Jewish practice as an extension of their liberal Protestant convictions. Over the years, they came to take on an exclusively Jewish identity. They represent the only instance of an entire community adopting Judaism without historic or genealogical ties to the tradition. While they once enjoyed substantial numbers, by the twentieth century only a remnant remained, all making their home in Bozodujfala. In this small village, people of all faiths frequently visited their neighbors' places of worship and celebrated one another's religious festivals.

In 1989, the Romanian communist dictator Nicolae Ceausescu finally approved a public works project that the residents of Bozodujfala had long anticipated: a flood-control dam in the local river. The villagers were doubly pleased with the news because the project would provide flood control as well as jobs to the poverty-stricken area.[82] But when construction began, they experienced a horrible shock. The project they were working on was not the one they had requested. The dam would not control flooding; instead, it would result in the complete flooding of the entire village. They had become a part of Ceausescu's plan to annihilate Hungarian ethnicity by destroying villages and forcibly relocating the people to tiny rooms in cinderblock housing developments, where they would be unable to maintain their cultural identity. When the villagers realized this, they tried to sabotage their work, but it was too late. The regime sent in Romanian troops to complete the project and evict the people. The villagers had to leave without time to remove their furniture or their animals. They did gather as an entire community for one last worship service at the Unitarian church. Today, you can visit Bozodujfala and see the eerie sight of the ruined steeples of the tallest churches rising from the middle of the artificial lake.[83]

The story of Martin and Jacob and the story of the ruined village are connected in several ways. In the intertwining of these stories we can see not only how early European Unitarians aspired to make meaningful connections with Jewish communities, but also how a variety of oppressions troubled this dream. The creative engagement between Judaism and Unitarianism in Eastern Europe did not end happily. What began in the mid-sixteenth century as both close and well-differentiated relationships between Unitarians and Jews were complicated by the end of the century by increases in both anti-Semitism and anti-Unitarian persecution. This pressure caused some Unitarians to distance themselves from Judaism for their own safety, but, interestingly, it also caused others to identify both with and as Jews.

Ruins of the Catholic church in the
flooded village of Bozodujfala

The most powerful of the forces that brought Martin Czechowic and Rabbi Jacob together began taking shape in 1492, a generation before their story unfolds. In that year, with anti-Semitism rising across Europe, Spanish Jews, who had previously thrived under a fairly generous tolerance, were given the choice of exile or conversion to Christianity. As discussed in chapter 1, Michael Servetus emerged from the resulting culture of New Christianity, in which many people of Jewish background took on a Christian identity, whether they converted for reasons of the heart or the sword. And while Servetus did not have a Jewish background himself, he had knowledge typical of a convert, including a deep understanding of Hebrew scripture as it was seen by Jewish scholars.

How could he have learned Hebrew and Jewish apologetics so thoroughly in a Spain supposedly left without any Jews? Even while the climate in Spain was grossly anti-Semitic, the growing interest in biblical studies allowed many conversos, some of whom still defined themselves as belonging to the line of Jewish sages, to enjoy profitable employment as teachers of Hebrew and Jewish scripture. Such studies prepared the ground for profound changes, including the emergence of anti-Trinitarianism.[84]

The radical potential of biblical studies became directly apparent in 1516, when Erasmus published his controversial Greek edition of the New Testament. He excluded from it what had been one of the most powerful proof texts of the Trinity, 1 John 5:8: "There are three on earth that bear record in Heaven: the Father, the Word, and the Holy Spirit and these three are one." Erasmus had demonstrated, through exacting historical scholarship, that this verse did not appear in the oldest available manuscripts, and hence argued that it was a late, spurious addition to scripture. While he excluded the passage on scholarly rather than theological grounds, his work made anti-Trinitarianism thinkable. Scholars alarmed by this tried to repair the damage by compiling lists of biblical terms suggestive of the Trinity, but these attempts often had the opposite effect of their intention. This work often just highlighted concerns about the integrity of retrospectively inserting the language of fourth-century doctrines of the Trinity into much older scripture.

Michael Servetus made the next move, deliberately uncoupling the Hebrew Bible from its later Christian interpretations. In 1542, while living in exile after escaping the Inquisition and working as an editor under the assumed name of Michel de Villeneuve, he re-released his 1528 edition of the Bible, this time complete with copious notes that, rather than treating the Old Testament as a prophetic anticipation of the Christian revelation, restored the Jewish scriptures to their own cultural and historical specificity. For example, Christians saw Isaiah 7:14 as prophesying the birth of Jesus, but instead of using the word "virgin," his edition offered "young woman," a more literal rendering of the Hebrew. He also omitted the annotations to the Song of Songs that Christian publishers used to suggest that the verses be read as love songs to Christ. Most scandalously, though, he wrote a note on Isaiah 53, which Christians commonly interpreted as a prophetic depiction of the sufferings of Jesus, explaining that the chapter actually referred to Cyrus, king of Persia.[85]

Later anti-Trinitarians inspired by Servetus thus inherited not only his skepticism about the Trinity, but respect for the independent authenticity of Judaism. Jews were not inferior versions of Christians; rather, each group had its own, equally valid revelation. Jacob Paleologus, a radical theologian of the Polish Unitarian church who was greatly inspired by Servetus, would eventually argue that Jesus's teaching did nothing to invalidate the Hebrew scriptures. In this view, Jesus did not come to offer Jews a radical new teaching because Judaism was no longer complete by itself; rather, Jesus had come as a Jew to ask the Jews to follow their own ethical code more closely.

For years the radical Protestants inspired by Servetus were isolated and on the run, moving around the continent in search of safety. Many eventually found refuge in Poland. A number of factors contributed to making Poland a safe place. Although it was a monarchy, a large nobility held power in a decentralized way, without internal distinctions of rank. Nobles who owned a few horses and one crumbling ancestral home had the same rank and privileges as those who controlled vast estates and many villages. All could grant tolerance and refuge to religious dissidents as they liked, and many became deeply interested in the new theologies. Most eventually identified as Protestant.

The Reformation in Poland had a radical flavor to it from the start. Lisamanio, the chaplain to the Polish queen Bona, began holding remarkably open discussions about Protestantism quite early. In 1546, a mysterious guest calling himself "Spiritus" (probably the Dutch radical Adam Pastor) dropped in on one such meeting to ask questions about the validity of Trinitarian doctrine. This episode took on the mythic status of an origin story when later Polish Unitarians wrote their history. Once the Reformed Church formally gathered, it too welcomed lively discussion. As early as 1556, anti-Trinitarian questions were raised in open synod, although they were not aggressively pursued.

Among the dissenters inspired by Servetus who made a home in Poland was Giorgio Biandrata, who would become a major figure in the Transylvanian Unitarian Church. Biandrata seems to have come to Eastern Europe not only for refuge, but with the explicit intention of establishing an international church movement based on the unity of God.[86] His subtle diplomatic skills proved quite effective in moving the Reformed Church in this direction, and he was able to craftily inject anti-Trinitarian ideas into critical religious debates in both Poland and Transylvania. While moderating a debate in 1562, for instance, he asked that the synod not use any theological language that was not biblically based. All willingly agreed, meaning that the concept of the Trinity was excluded from the start and the debate effectively thrown to the anti-Trinitarians.

Despite its liberalism, the Polish government was not entirely complacent about these radical theological developments, and in 1564 the foreign anti-Trinitarian agitators were expelled from Poland

and forced into exile once again. But the seeds were already well sown. In 1565 Trinitarians frustrated with the continuing debate walked away from the synod, and those left behind became the Minor Reformed Church of Poland, formed around an explicitly Unitarian theology. And one of the first things this newly gathered body did was to enter into serious conversations with its Jewish neighbors.

Although members of the Minor Reformed Church did not always agree about the nature of Jesus, they were all interested in pursuing a dialog with Judaism. Some church historians classify some of these anti-Trinitarians as "Judaizers" or "semi-Judaizers." These terms are problematic, as they have a history of being employed in anti-Semitic ways. But they do reflect the way that many radical Reformation figures deliberately moved toward Judaism. Protestants attempting to return to the earliest form of Christianity, before it had been contaminated by imperial concerns, church hierarchy, and later additions to the creed, were naturally interested in the practices and beliefs that would have been Jesus's own. For this reason, they sometimes adopted aspects of Jewish religious practice into their own observances. Even those who did not felt that, as advocates of the unity of God, they were close kin to Jews, and so, although they differentiated themselves from both Judaism and Judaizers, they did not do so antagonistically.

Martin Czechowic earned for himself the nickname "Rabbi of Lublin" for his interest in developing conversations with the Jewish community. Through this interest he met Rabbi Jacob. As early as 1569, Rabbi Jacob and other Jewish leaders were active and welcome participants in the meetings of the Unitarians, and Jacob and Martin met frequently to debate and discuss theology together. Their friendship grew. In 1575, Czechowic published a book of arguments against Judaism and efforts to Judaize Christianity that grew out of his conversations with his friend. Jacob responded in kind, publishing a response not long afterward. While both men strongly defended their traditions, they treated one another with mutual interest and respect.

But then something changed. First, Jacob noticed that his old friend was ignoring him, no longer inviting him to debate. He wondered if this avoidance had to do with a rumor about Czechowic soon publishing a new book more hostile to Jacob and Judaism than his earlier one. Jacob confronted him and Czechowic responded, denying responsibility for the breach in their relationship:

> I did not prohibit you from corresponding with me orally as well as in writing. A long time ago, I had already asked you, not only through the brother of Marcin, the tailor, and others, but also through the Jew of Lublin and myself personally, that you should at least send me your composition. . . . Some people told me that you are writing against me. Also, I heard that you would like to attend the synod and converse with me. I waited for this with joy. But of the fact that you would want to debate me, nobody told me.[87]

The rumor of a hostile new tome proved true. In 1581, Czechowic published a rebuttal to Jacob's book that demonstrated nothing of his previous polite regard. The book brutally indicted Judaism, ridiculing what Czechowic called a Jewish predilection for meaningless superstitions. Moreover, Czechowic had earlier asserted that Jesus was the greatest of all prophets, but finally entirely human. In the new book, Czechowic expressed an adorationist theology: while he still believed that Jesus was born human, he now argued that he had been elevated to a kind of divinity through God's unique adoption of him as his son, and that he was therefore properly an object of adoration, or worship.

Standard histories of the Polish church claim that Czechowic was always an adorationist, and that there had always been tension in the anti-Trinitarian movement between adorationists and those who held that Jesus was strictly human. To an extent this is true, but the statement masks the radical changes that took place not only in Czechowic's own thought but also in the movement as a whole.

For example, one of the earliest gatherings of anti-Trinitarians, the Council of Venice in 1550, rejected adorationism in favor of a much more radical Judaizing theology. According to this view, Jesus was one of several human children born to human parents, and while his unselfishness made him a worthy model for emulation, he played no role in the salvation of others. Individuals are saved by, and rewarded for, their own good works, and those not saved are not condemned to hell, but simply die with their bodies.[88] While this theology was accepted at the Council of Venice, by the later part of the sixteenth century it had become an extremist position in an increasingly adorationist church.

The most tragic divide between Unitarian adorationists and Judaizers came in Transylvania, in the form of a split between two other old friends, the leaders of the Transylvanian church: Francis David and Giorgio Biandrata. Francis David was a native of Transylvania, a man with a restless and energetic mind, who in the course of his life converted from Catholicism to Lutheranism (in which he served as superintendent), to Reform Calvinism (in which he also held a leadership role), and finally to Unitarianism. His conversion to Unitarianism had everything to do with his relationship with Giorgio Biandrata, who had deliberately cultivated David as he sought to gather a church around what had previously only been the theology of anti-Trinitarianism. For years the two collaborated in debating other traditions, and they served together in the Transylvanian royal court, where Biandrata was physician and Francis David, largely through Biandrata's influence, court preacher.

Both men changed their understanding of the nature of Jesus over the years. When the Unitarian king John Sigismund died in a somewhat suspicious hunting accident in 1571, official tolerance of Unitarianism was no longer certain, and Unitarians were eventually removed from high public and court office. Sigismund's successor to the throne, Stephen Bathori, declared in 1572 that Unitarianism would remain legal only if it introduced no further theological innovations. For a young tradition open to new thought and continuous revelation, this requirement represented a horrible bind. Biandrata, ever the diplomat, responded by attempting to re-entrench himself and the church in the less controversial, adorationist, Christ-centered form of Unitarianism. Francis David was less cautious.

David's own theology became increasingly progressive, partially due to the influence of some of the radical theologians who had taken refuge in Transylvania. Many of these scholars, including Jacob Paleologus and Adam Neuser, had relocated on David's invitation, with a modest but good living teaching at the Unitarian school in Kolosvar already secured for them. As a result of these influences and his own tendency to push against theological boundaries, David become more and more of a Judaizer. To Biandrata's great horror, David began publicly advocating that the Unitarian Church cease addressing prayers to Jesus at all, an obvious innovation that would place the church dangerously outside the law.

Things came to a head in 1578, when Biandrata and David debated each other on this issue in front of 322 Unitarian pastors. David argued quite persuasively that worshipping Jesus was a form of idolatry, and he seemed to carry the day. But the dispute didn't end there. Matthew Vehe-Glirius rushed to Transylvania from Germany to help reinforce David's side. A scholar of both academic Jewish life and Jewish communities, Vehe-Glirius brought to Transylvania a highly Judaized Unitarianism. Judaizing Unitarians typically held that the New Testament did not supplant Hebrew scripture, but Vehe-Glirius went further, arguing that the New Testament was actually far less inspired than the Old Testament. After all, he argued, Jesus had completely failed to bring about the Kingdom of God in his lifetime, as he seemed to have promised. In this way, Jesus could be seen as an unsuccessful prophet. Accordingly, Christians should continue to respect Jewish scripture and practice. Vehe-Glirius also thought it appropriate for Unitarians to declare Saturday as the day of worship and follow Jewish dietary laws.

Panicked about the political implications of such radicalism, Biandrata took strong measures. He was concerned that Unitarianism would find itself on the wrong side of the law both by proposing such innovations and by identifying with Judaism, itself not yet legally tolerated. He invited Faustus Socinus, a moderate adorationist and eminent theologian for the Polish movement, to come to Transylvania in order to talk sense into David. Socinus actually lived with David for a while, but in spite of Socinus's daily appeals, David refused to modify either his theology or his very public expression of it.

In 1579 Biandrata lost all hope of persuading David to moderate his views. In a desperate move to sacrifice David but save the church, he used his political connections to have David arrested for innovation. David was sentenced to a most horrible prison where, broken, ill, and denied medical attention, he soon died. Biandrata then called the Unitarian ministers into council and contrived the removal of David's most vocal followers. He also forced the council to pass a new and strongly adorationist platform. Biandrata, ever ambitious for the future of Unitarianism, felt that only such a platform would be both widely acceptable and safe enough to serve as the foundation of an international Unitarian Church.

The trauma in Transylvania had an immediate effect on the Polish church. Facing a political climate that was becoming increasingly hostile to Judaism, the Polish church sought likewise to expunge non-adorationist, Judaizing elements. Some, like the progressive theologian and Judaizer Simon Bundy, were actually excommunicated. And many who were already at least mildly adorationist, such as Czechowic, solidified their commitment to adorationism and withdrew from dialog with the Jewish community. The non-adorationist Unitarian point of view survived longer in Lithuania, where Rabbi Isaac ben Abraham had established relationships with Unitarians such as Paleologus and Budny. Rabbi Isaac's major book, *Faith Strengthened* (1585), speaks approvingly of the Unitarian respect for Judaism and the Hebrew scriptures.[89]

And yet even in Lithuania the Judaizing impulse did not survive much longer, beset as it was by increasing anti-Semitism and persecution.

So what to make of both the profundity and brevity of the hopes of Eastern European Unitarians to live in close relationship with their Jewish kin? To answer this, we will need to return to the connection between the dissolution of Czechowic and Jacob's friendship with the submerged village of Bozodujfala.

When the followers of Francis David were cast out beyond the fold of the Unitarian Church, some formed separately as Sabbatarians, adopting many Jewish practices. It was this group that over the years would transform into the Szekely Jews. Other followers of David kept their Unitarian identification, not publicly quarrelling with the official adorationist platform, but nonetheless coming to personally adopt some Jewish practices and rituals. This dynamic was hardly a secret, with the Jesuit Possevino observing in 1583 that the majority of Unitarian ministers in Eastern Transylvania did not eat pork.[90] By 1600 Sabbatarianism itself was clearly a separate religion, and yet as it was not a tolerated religion, many of its adherents maintained their official membership with the Unitarian Church.

In 1618, Prince Gabriel Bethen saw an opportunity to wreak havoc on both the Sabbatarians and the Unitarians by forcing the Unitarians to promise that they would weed out the Sabbatarians from their membership books. Panicked by the scrutiny, Sabbatarians and others who did not want to attract government attention transferred their membership to the Reformed Church. They survived in remote villages in Szeklerland in eastern Hungary, where they sometimes enjoyed the protection of powerful landowners, and gradually became the Szekely Jews. Nonetheless, by the mid-eighteenth century only one community survived, in the village of Bozodujfala, and we know its fate.

It is impossible to say when they began seeing themselves not as radically Judaizing Unitarians but as wholly Jewish. They declared their Jewish identity in 1867, the first year in which Judaism was legally tolerated. Geza Szavai, who grew up in the village before the government flooded it, writes that oppression solidified his identification as a Jew. "To become a Jew or to be a Jew must be a very complicated issue. But to be made a Jew—that is very easy. I was made a Jew."[91]

Historians often call this community of people who, uniquely, chose Judaism a happy result of creative Jewish and Unitarian interchange. That it certainly was. And yet the suppression of the Judaized form of Unitarianism is extremely sad. Its loss also obscured the understanding of Unitarianism as a liberal Christianity that holds as one of its highest values its kinship with Judaism and Islam.

History, of course, unfolds in ironic ways, and contemporary Unitarianism Universalism is definitely more Judaizing than not, and less adorationist. Even the contemporary Hungarian Unitarian church has come to agree with Francis David's cry that "God is One." Most people believe that this Unitarian slogan maintains the unity of God in defiance of Trinitarianism, but it was originally directed against the adorationists by the Judaizing Unitarians.[92] And although adorationism seemed to win the day in the sixteenth century, contemporary North American Unitarian Universalist congregations often not only are non-adorationist in theology, but also include many members with Jewish backgrounds. Even under great oppression, hybrid identities remain possible, waiting to emerge again another day.

FOUR

NORTH AMERICAN UNITARIANISM IN RELATIONSHIP TO ISLAM AND JUDAISM

As we have seen, the ideal of expressing multi-religious identities was an important, although sometimes subterranean, part of European Unitarianism. Until very recently, North American Unitarianism has been far less inclined toward multi-religious kinship. If indeed there is something inherently multi-religious about Unitarianism, the American version of the faith did much to repress such tendencies.

One significant difference between European and American Unitarianism was that American theology was more Arminian, while the European was more Arian. This meant the Europeans emphasized the unity of God to a greater extent, connecting them more closely to Jewish and Islamic monotheisms. Arianism suggests a focus on the theological issues related to the fourth-century bishop Arius, a distinct anti-Trinitarianism historically coupled with a concern for toleration. Strangely, American Unitarians willingly accepted the label of Arian when their enemies hurled it at them as Unitarianism emerged from Congregationalism, but it is largely a misnomer. More characteristic of American Unitarianism was Arminianism, named after the Dutch theologian Jacob

Arminius (1560–1609). In contrast to Calvinist notions of pre-destination, Arminians stress the importance of human free will and choice in accepting the grace that leads to salvation. In the left wing of the Congregationalist church, which eventually became Unitarian, this emphasis led to a corresponding trust in reason and our capacity to discern and choose good. And while William Ellery Channing did make explicitly anti-Trinitarian arguments in his 1819 sermon outlining the Unitarian platform, these were not the issues that drove the liberalization of the church. Nor did they result from concerns that the Trinity might be offensive to other faiths, as they did in Europe. Rather, they were a consequence of the new historical and critical approaches to scripture. Indeed, Channing and his generation were horrified when they were first called "Unitarians"—they were sure that they were not like the anti-Trinitarian English Unitarians, who did not revere Christ enough. And yet Arminianism alone does not adequately explain the difference in multi-religious engagement between North America and Europe. British Unitarians, themselves distinctly Arminian, showed a fair appetite for multi-religious encounter. Moreover, it sheds no light on the fascinating developments within contemporary North American Unitarian Universalism.

More people than ever are identifying as Jewish and Muslim Unitarian Universalists, and more of these people than ever consider themselves to be actively practicing both sides of a double faith. Linda Weltner, for instance, describes Unitarian Universalism as a place to which she can "bring" her Jewishness even as she celebrates belonging to her new community. For her, Unitarian Universalism provides a hospitable home for "multiple religious affiliations."[93] An increasing number of Muslim Unitarian Universalists echo these sentiments. These changes suggest that an older and more radical Unitarian commitment to multi-religious inclusivity may be resurfacing in the American church. Indeed, the historian Jerome Friedman has noted that contemporary American Unitarian Universalist membership reflects Jewish-Christian mixed identities in ways that resemble the Eastern European historical past more than the American church's own inheritance.[94]

Two closely related elements of that inheritance have historically dampened the development of a more robust inclusivity. One is the tendency to greatly restrict church membership, inherited from the Puritan congregationalism's covenantal theology; the other is the social location of the early North American Unitarians.

Unitarianism, like the Congregationalism from which it emerged, comprised competing ideas of how inclusive a religious tradition should be. The early Congregationalists in this country tightly controlled membership in the church, as did all the churches that separated from the Church of England. The church of this world was the Visible Church, and it was important that the Visible Church reflect as perfectly as possible the Invisible Church (heaven and its population). The covenant of membership was restricted: the point of Puritanism was that the righteous and the wicked did not have to share in church membership together, as they did in the more promiscuous English parish system. The original system of covenant was the mechanism by which a parsimonious clergy and a small number of especially pious church members limited church membership to select people. Those who wished to join had to give clear indications, through accounts of their conversion experience and evidence of their Christian living, that they were saints—preordained for salvation.

Contemporary Unitarian Universalists commonly suggest that our current covenantal organization is directly inherited from our Puritan past. But this is misleading, because our current understanding of covenant is that covenant is what allows us to hold our doors open to a diversity of peoples and theologies. We now think of covenant as a mechanism for inclusion, and think of church as a voluntary association of people who have freely (and without facing meaningful obstacles) elected to participate together in a gathered body. That we can think this at all points to another current at work in the early Congregational church beyond the merely restrictive one.

The sharp restriction on the number of church members partly caused the eventual decline of the Puritan way, as the system depended on a vast number of people who were denied membership to nonetheless support, respect, and even attend church. Additionally, many first-generation Puritans faced a difficult dilemma: they were church members themselves, but their children were denied the benefits of membership until they could qualify for it—if they ever did. This famously led to the adoption of a category of partial church membership in the Half-Way Covenant of 1662, which allowed children of church members the sacrament of baptism (but not communion or a vote in church affairs).

Many lay people also creatively and determinedly misinterpreted the messages they were receiving from their ministers and teachers about the restrictiveness of covenant, construing sermons that were meant to be fearsome in the most positive way possible. They attended church but did not make it the focus of their lives; indeed, they were called "horseshed Christians" because, between the two Sunday services, they would gather in the shed to discuss secular matters such as farming. They derived adequate religious comfort not from the clergy or senior laity or through their membership in the church, but from their own satisfaction with their well-intentioned, if less than rigorous, personal devotions.[95] As church historian David Hall writes, "theirs was a faith less rooted in ongoing anxiety than in an ethics of 'weaned affections,' and though they may have wondered if this was 'hypocrisy,' as some ministers suggested in their sermons, they were willing in most cases to accept one another's practice as sincere."[96]

In any case, two opposing groups eventually developed in the church: those, largely supported by the clergy, who wished membership to be more tightly controlled and the piety of members guaranteed, and those, largely but not exclusively lay people, who demanded that the doors of the church be opened to all those willing to participate. Indeed, the struggle for the "power of the keys"—the authority to determine who might be allowed into membership—was the primary source of tensions and outright conflict between Congregationalist clergy and their people for generations leading up to the "Unitarian Departure."[97] By the dawn of Unitarianism in the early nineteenth century, liberal and conservative Congregationalists alike could easily agree that church membership had become so widely available that it could no longer be seen as the earthly indication of a sure state of salvation.

This made conservatives anxious about the state of common doctrine; in the past, the strict requirements for church membership, though they did not include a creedal test, had ensured doctrinal conformity. To be able to state one's relationship to the doctrine of grace that superseded the doctrine of church membership, one had to be quite conversant in orthodox Puritan theology. And indeed, most of the confessions of faith offered by would-be members conformed closely to established ideas of salvation. Now, worried conservatives attempted to work creedal affirmations, especially regarding the Trinity, into their church covenants. Liberals, in the meantime, tended to celebrate the theological diversity of a more inclusive church covenant, and they effectively dismantled the Puritan theology: They no longer considered church membership synonymous with salvation, and saw both as far more wide-reaching, inclusive, and readily available than had any other generation of New Englanders. This liberal misreading of covenant both allowed Unitarianism to form and became its hallmark. Even this inclusiveness, however, remained restrained by other factors.

Having emerged out of the established, state-supported church, North American Unitarianism developed a comfort with the social and political status quo unknown to the Unitarian movements in Europe. While Unitarians here approached and perhaps even (with some caution) crossed theological borders, they were otherwise quite well grounded in an intrinsically conservative public sphere that afforded them many privileges they were reluctant to relinquish. So what cultural and social position, exactly, did American

Unitarianism hold? My favorite image of it comes from Perry Miller, that delightfully arch historian of the New England Puritans. After writing about the failure of American theologians after Jonathan Edwards to fill the old bottle of Calvinism with a new wine worthy of the interest of the younger generation, he goes on to mention a brand new vintage: "Unitarianism was an entirely different wine from any that had ever been pressed from the grapes of Calvinism, and in entirely new bottles, which the merchants of Boston found much to their liking. It was a pure, white dry claret that went well with dinners served by the Harvard Corporation, but it was mild and guaranteed not to send them home reeling and staggering."[98]

Within American Protestantism, one's relationship to "reeling and staggering" turns out to be quite important. To stagger and reel openly would group one with the old enemies of the New England Puritans, the Antinomians. Puritans famously dismissed as Antinomian those who, like Anne Hutchinson and the Quakers, felt that their inward connection with God was strong and sure enough to justify defying human law when it went against their conscience. The Puritans frequently employed the metaphor of drunkenness to explain the danger of relying on direct personal inspiration, noting that "like strong wine, it makes men's judgments to reel and stagger," causing them to be drunk with imagined revelations.[99]

The Puritans, of course, hated the disorder that could be wrought upon society by people (especially women) claiming a religious truth independent of the church, the state, social convention, or reason, at least as it was defined by established authorities. Nor were their objections merely prudish and controlling, as people today too often assume. The New England elders were building a community and a nation, and they saw that such claims would lead to fractiousness and a variety of irresponsible individualisms, many of which trouble Unitarian Universalism still.

Yet while they understood its dangers, it was the Puritans themselves who first brewed the dangerous Antinomian wine, even if they managed to keep it tightly corked. At the heart of New England Calvinism was a deeply mystical vein which taught that all true believers might be completely regenerated in Christ through faith alone. This suggestion that divinity moved within and transformed the individual soul was tempered by strict doctrines of original sin and predestination, but it was there.

This is important to our story because Unitarianism in many ways inherited both the Puritan-inspired sense of indwelling divinity and the Puritan impulse toward restraint. Puritans and Unitarians were both averse to staggering and reeling, but among the Unitarians, who were not required to adhere to a creed, a new tempering force was in effect: a class and racial location that conflated the social good with the status quo. What was once held at bay by inflexible doctrines was now controlled by the very fineness of that white claret. The inherent tensions of this arrangement do much to explain some of the ambivalences of American Unitarian identity, so well captured by Daniel Walker Howe: "[The nineteenth-century Unitarians were] men of many paradoxes. Religious liberals and social conservatives, at once optimistic and apprehensive, nationalistic and cosmopolitan, they were elitists in a land dedicated to equality, proponents of freedom of conscience who supported a religious establishment, and reformers who feared change."[100]

But when speaking of Unitarian social location, we should be both extremely cautious and extremely specific. As theologian Thandeka points out, contemporary Unitarian Universalists tend to take an odd and unhelpful pleasure in overstating our historical class situation, inventing rich ancestors as a hedge against what was actually considerable financial precariousness.[101] Also, we must not assume that Unitarians have consistently been of a certain class across historical periods. Many, if not most, of the congregations founded in the period between the Civil War and the Great Depression included members across the class spectrum, even though they did tend to be founded by wealthy people.

And even the upward shift in class demographics that occurred under Samuel Atkins Eliot's presidency of the American Unitarian Association (1937–58) was not unmixed.[102] While Eliot did stop funding congregations that could not sustain themselves, focusing denominational resources instead on the establishment of lay-led fellowships in college towns, these new fellowships were most often located near fairly humble colleges, and their membership could hardly be considered upper class. And even though American Unitarians in the early nineteenth century did represent a relatively privileged class, branding them simply as elite misses how theirs was a negotiated privilege, and therefore always somewhat precarious. Specifically, much of early nineteenth-century Unitarianism represented a marriage between families with money and families with pedigree. People of great economic but little cultural capital established mutually beneficial alliances with people of cultural but little economic capital.[103] These arrangements allowed clergy to negotiate the loss of status that came with the disestablishment of the church and the consequent loss of tax revenue as a source of support.

As gifted historians have chronicled, one way that the liberal clergy responded to multiple diminishments of their political and religious roles and their social prestige was by promoting their cultural and literary credentials, strategically moving their field of influence to include literature.[104] Historians such as Ann Douglas claim that this move backfired because it forced ministers to form alliances with women. The production and consumption of religious and popular literature was considered a feminine endeavor, and their association with it, Douglas argues, banished the ministers even further from realms of serious (masculine) influence. Yet the liberal ministers largely succeeded in establishing themselves not only as purveyors of literary culture but also in other positions of useful influence. Clergymen often served as the administrators of new philanthropic organizations funded by mercantile money. They recommended titles for their congregants' empty libraries in their brand new Beacon Hill mansions, helping to provide those establishments with a veneer of culture. Eventually the marriage of financial and intellectual culture became literal, as when wealthy nineteenth-century merchants began to encourage the marriage of their daughters to liberal men with cultural and intellectual accomplishments but no significant fortune.

The British nineteenth-century novelist Elizabeth Gaskell brilliantly portrays a similar dynamic in England. In *North and South*, a presumably Unitarian minister is forced to surrender the living offered by his bucolic southern parish and relocate to the northern industrial town of Manchester. He trades on his cultural and intellectual capital in order to scratch out a living. He gives public lectures on the classics to workingmen and private lessons to the mill owners and operators, who, while intelligent, lack liberal education. Meanwhile, his daughter starts a romance with one of the mill operators, even though she is horrified by what she sees as his immoral exploitation of his workers. To her credit, she also establishes real connections with the area's poor. Nonetheless, in the course of the romantic relationship, she learns to subtly adjust her idealism to the pragmatics of industry. The mill operator, meanwhile, by virtue of his relationship with her, develops an interest in bettering himself. He take steps to improve his relationship with his workers, solidifying his position with them without having to dramatically improve their material conditions.

This narrative encapsulates the best and the worst of Unitarian social ethics. On the one hand, Unitarian ethics were open enough to adapt to changing circumstances. Naive idealism could be modified by pragmatism, creating space for real, if not revolutionary, changes. On the other hand, this sort of negotiation did require and result from a complicity with, and even dependence on, cultural and economic privilege. The historian Peter Field puts this in the bleakest possible way, saying that the Boston Brahmin clergy "transformed God's covenant with the Puritan nation into a class compact with a privileged elite."[105] But he too overstates the case.

The alliance of cultural and economic capital was not a permanent agreement, but a negotiated and changeable settlement that would have been void if Unitarian leaders staggered and reeled over too many significant class, political, or racial lines.

An anecdote from the life of the Universalist George de Benneville illustrates how many divides would have to be crossed if an elite white eighteenth-century American were interested in engaging with Muslims. De Benneville, who practiced his Universalist ministry in Pennsylvania from 1741 to 1793, went to sea at the age of twelve; when his ship docked in Algiers he encountered Moors for the first time. "Moor" is a derisive and racialized term applied by Europeans, often rather loosely, to Berber and Arab Muslims from the Iberian Peninsula, what was formerly al-Andalus. De Benneville used the term to describe Algerians, making it clear that even by the eighteenth century it was used as a racialized category for all Muslims.[106]

Several of these Moors had just come aboard de Benneville's ship with food and drink for the sailors when one of them fell and injured his leg. De Benneville was revolted by what he thought was his companions' excessively emotional reaction: two of them fell to the deck alongside their friend, kissed his wound, shed copious tears over it, and then cried loudly, apparently to the sun. De Benneville confronted them with their heathen silliness, only to have them tell him that they kissed their wounded companion's leg in sympathy, that they shed tears so that their salt would clean the wound, and that they cried to the sun so that its creator would have compassion and heal him quickly.

This experience converted de Benneville to an explicitly multi-religious belief in universal salvation. He cried out, "Are these men Heathens? No; I confess before God they are Christians, and I myself a Heathen! Behold the first conviction that the grace of our Sovereign Good employed: he was pleased to convince a white person by blacks, one who carried the name of a Christian, by a Pagan, and who was obliged to confess himself a Heathen." The Unitarian theologian Thandeka has written movingly of de Benneville's highly embodied conversion experience: "His mind did not transform him; his body did. His tears, pounding heart, and torrential feelings constituted a revelation that challenged the racial, class, and religious creeds that were core to his self-concept." She highlights aspects of de Benneville's character that would have been unusual among proto-Unitarian Congregationalists of his generation: his openness to a dramatic conversion process, his trust of embodied experience, his capacity for radically revising his sense of self, and his willingness to suspend rational thought and be guided by powerful emotion.

Perhaps, then, we should not be surprised that it is not until the advent of nineteenth-century Transcendentalism that we find Unitarians expressing much interest in Islam. Even then, they engaged with books, including translations of sacred texts and travelers' accounts, rather than with actual communities or people. The Transcendentalists did help to originate the American habit of looking to the East for philosophical and literary inspiration and for enduring spiritual truths not compromised by modernity. Before the end of the nineteenth century many Unitarians were both producing and using collections of texts from a variety of world religions, including Islam. Dissatisfaction with contemporary expressions of Christianity and with the growing influences of industrialism partially fed this Orientalist quest, as did the destabilization of the Bible's authority by historical criticism.[107]

The infamous weakness of the Transcendentalist- and Unitarian-inspired approaches to Islam and other world traditions was their tendency to borrow from these traditions without attending to their cultural specificity. Indeed, both approaches tended to be interested in the texts of other religions precisely because they imagined that they communicated a deep truth that was independent of historical or cultural location. As Arthur Versluis has pointed out, "for many Transcendentalists, Saadi, Hafiz, and other Islamic poets represented literary or poetic interchangeability."[108] Emily Mace, who has done interesting work on the use of world religious materials in Unitarian personal and corporate worship, argues against the charge that the use of such decontextualized materials was necessarily appropriative, hegemonic, and imperialistic. She asserts that these collections went a long way toward overcoming prejudice and creating sympathy for different traditions.[109] But it is fairly clear that interest in the texts did not translate into a passion for conversation with actual Muslims.

One of the most successful anthologies of Eastern religious texts was *The Poetry of the East*, published by the Unitarian minister William Alger in 1856. A year later Alger followed it up with an article in the *Christian Examiner* titled "The Piety and the Poetry of the Islamic Sufis." Alger's understanding of Sufism was rather incomplete, and, not surprisingly, he removes the Sufi texts from their Islamic context and rewrites them as expressions of a universal romantic mysticism. Alger was especially fond of the thirteenth-century Sufi poet Jalal al-Din ar-Rumi, and there is much evidence that the contemporary American interest in Rumi's poetry—heavily rewritten and decontextualized—originated with Alger.[110] But, for all his Orientalism, Alger was quite sympathetic to Islam, and after a brief but fascinating warning against falling too deeply for what he explicitly names Oriental Antinomianism, he suggests that the practice of Sufism might provide interested Unitarians with a welcome spiritual depth. He writes in oddly suggestive language that the Sufis can help "lead us to a state of faith and fruition, that healthy state of full Christian piety wherein we feel, in oft and favored hours, a rapture of calmness, a vision of heaven, a perfect communion of the Father, confessing with electric shudders of awe and joy the motions of the Spirit as the hand of God wanders solemnly among the chords of the heart."[111] However, there is no evidence that any Unitarians took up Sufism as a result of this exciting recommendation.

Indeed, the only account we have of nineteenth-century Unitarians directly exploring Islam is from a dubious if fascinating source: Orestes Brownson, the Universalist turned Unitarian minister, founding member of the Transcendentalist Club, and later convert to Catholicism. In his autobiography, *The Convert,* he claims that he was frustrated with Unitarian Transcendentalism because it had moved from drawing inspiration from other religious traditions to practicing them. He writes that

> there were those among us who openly claimed the Mahometans as good Unitarians, and were quite disposed to fraternize with them. . . . One of the most brilliant and gifted of the early Unitarian ministers of Boston actually did go to Turkey, turn Mahometan, and become a Moslem preacher. He published in English a volume of Mahometan sermons, which I once read. I thought them equal to most Unitarian sermons I had seen or heard.[112]

No traces of such a book have been found, and of course, the fact that Brownson does not name the minister suggests hyperbole. But his maligning of Unitarianism as a gateway to Islamic conversion is interesting in itself. Perhaps it is not surprising that here, as in Transylvania, it is those most frightened of multireligious engagement who can most freely read it as a natural expression of Unitarian identity.

At least one person in the late nineteenth-century American liberal religious circle did actually not only engage with living Muslims but also convert to Islam; this was Alexander Russell Webb, author of *Islam in America* (1893).[113] An American diplomat who spent time serving in the Philippines, he was also acquainted with Muslims in India and Burma, although his interest in Islam and other world traditions predated his travels. Webb was not Unitarian, although he seemed to see similarities between the particulars of Unitarianism and Islam, where his American Unitarian contemporaries saw Islam only as one more example of the eternal truth. Webb saw an appealing "Unitarian monotheism" in Islam, and when he started his journal *The Moslem World,* he marketed it specifically to "Mussulmans, Unitarians, and Non-Sectarians."[114] But his attempts to introduce Islam to America amounted, finally, to very little. Many people found him a ludicrous figure, expounding on Islam in his red fez, and newspapers denounced his attempts at Islamic "propagandizing" and "proselytizing" as both ineffectual and offensive.[115]

Unitarian engagement with Islam since the nineteenth century continues to exhibit the same tendency toward Orientalist curiosity, occasionally mixed with withdrawal, especially when Unitarianism has been attacked for teaching an inferior version of Islam under the guise of liberal Christianity. It is only since the beginning of this century, and especially after the terrorist events of September 11, 2001, that Unitarian Universalists have begun to engage directly with Muslim communities. In a show of solidarity, the president of the Unitarian Universalist Association at the time, Rev. William Sinkford, visited the American Muslim Council after the attacks, the first non-Muslim ever to do so; and shortly thereafter the UUA asked congregations to stand in solidarity with Muslims. When Sikhs were mistaken for Muslims and violently abused, UUs were asked to stand with that community as well. The congregation in Detroit stood guard outside a nearby mosque during prayers and gatherings; the Portland congregation wrapped their building in a banner proclaiming their support for their Arab and Muslim neighbors and friends.[116] And yet in all of this there was no expression of any particular affinity between Islam and Unitarianism, just concern that Islamic people were being unfairly treated, together with the interest in eternal truth that was by now more than 150 years old. In 2008 the UUA's Washington Office for Advocacy issued the pamphlet *Unitarian Universalists and Islam: An Introduction to Interfaith Dialogue and Reading Group Guide.* Under the heading "Why Work with Muslims in Particular?" it mainly said this: "Their experiences with the Transcendent Divine can teach us more about how we can commune with the universe."[117]

ॐ

American Unitarian interactions with Judaism, in contrast, focused on the particularities of Jewish identity, owing partly to Unitarianism's Puritan past. The sixteenth- and seventeenth-century Puritans had an odd relationship to Jewish identity; they mostly appropriated it for themselves, and then used the remnant of that appropriation to define Jews as radically and racially "other." They believed that, like Moses, they were carrying out God's "errand into the wilderness," and that they were in North America to build the New Jerusalem. In this scenario, the Puritans, not the Jews, were now God's chosen people. Consequently, many Puritans became frantic to convert Jews to Christianity, both to show that the covenant had been transferred and to mark the onset of the promised end times.

Consider, for instance, the powerful Puritan divine Cotton Mather. In 1696 he was completing his *Magnalia Christi americana*, his famous history of the founding of the Massachusetts Bay Colony. Using the strongest possible biblical and mythic language, he retold the stories of the Hebrew Bible with the Puritans cast in the lead, and numbered himself among Israel's great prophets, a veritable Moses. At the same time he began to wear a skullcap while working and to refer to himself as Rabbi Mather, and he devoted his minimal spare time to writing rather desperate polemics aimed at converting actual American Jews, of whom there were not many in the New World. He even wrote an entire book in a failed attempt to convert just one Jewish family.[118]

Having appropriated Jewish religious, but not racial, identity for themselves, the Puritans next wondered who might be racially, but not religiously, Jewish. Many of them could not resist the temptation to think of Native Americans as racial Jews—descendants of a lost tribe of Israel.[119] "Lost tribe" theories have waxed and waned in popularity in American history, some persisting even into the nineteenth century, when a few archaeologists still tried to find traces of Hebrew verses on Native artifacts.

American Unitarianism did not adopt this Puritan blurring of Jewish and Native identities, and historians Daniel McKanan and Daniel Buchanan have shown how Unitarians and other religious liberals have struggled with the legacy of Puritan violence toward Native Americans.[120] Yet early North American Unitarians sometimes appropriated Jewish identity much as the Puritans did. These appropriations in some ways draw Unitarianism closer to Judaism, but at the same time they entrench an essential sense of difference, not between Unitarianism and Judaism, but between Unitarians and Jews.

Consider, as an odd but intriguing example, the case of Henry Adams (1838–1918). Raised within the circle of Bostonian Unitarian privilege, he eventually stopped identifying as a Unitarian, although he often still spoke as a Unitarian insider. Indeed, his work frequently plays a privileged sense of belonging against a claim to outsider status, such as when he famously denounces the smugness of Unitarianism in *The Education of Henry Adams*:

> Nothing quieted doubt so completely as the mental calm of the Unitarian clergy. In uniform excellence of life and character, moral and intellectual, the score of Unitarian clergymen about Boston, who controlled society and Harvard College, were never excelled. They proclaimed as their merit that they insisted on no doctrine, but taught, or tried to teach, the means of leading a virtuous, useful, unselfish life, which they held to be sufficient for salvation. For them, difficulties might be ignored; doubts were waste of thought; nothing exacted solution. Boston had solved the universe; or had offered and realized the best solution yet tried. The problem was worked out.[121]

Scholars seeking to understand Adams's curious relationship with Judaism have paid particular attention to his sense of having been born to a privileged tribe. As a young man he demonstrated a progressive and distinctively anti-racist opposition to anti-Semitism. But by the mid-1890s, in the wake of the economic meltdown of 1893, his letters reveal a growing anti-Semitic obsession. In attempting to understand this change in attitude, scholars have turned to the opening of *The Education:*

> In the third house below Mount Vernon Place, February 16, 1838, a child was born, and christened later by his uncle, the minister of the First Church after the tenets of Boston Unitarianism, as Henry Brooks Adams.

Had he been born in Jerusalem under the shadow of the Temple and circumcised in the Synagogue by his uncle the high priest, under the name of Israel Cohen, he would scarcely have been more distinctly branded, and not much more heavily handicapped in the races of the coming century.[122]

There is a curious blend here of a denial of privilege and a claim to be disadvantaged by it. Also, his appropriation of Jewish identity to make the point is troubling. And while Adams's attitude cannot be said to be shared across Unitarianism, a curious sense did emerge among Unitarians early on (and persist into the twentieth century) that a new age might be at hand, if only Jews would stop insisting so hard on maintaining the distinctness of their identity.

Consider Joseph Priestly's curious blend of multi-religious interest and appropriation of Jewish identity. He was one of the few Unitarians to show much interest in world religions before the Transcendentalist era, perhaps a result of his more European style of faith. In his 1770 publication *An Appeal to the Serious and Candid Professors of Christianity*, Priestly, in moves reminiscent of Michael Servetus, suggests that Judaism, Islam, and Christianity are close kin because of their shared emphasis on the unity of God. He furthermore argues that Unitarian churches should be founded to preserve this kinship:

> the great offence to Jews, Mahometans, and the world at large, being the doctrine of the Trinity, it is highly necessary that societies of Christians should be formed expressly on this principle of the Divine Unity, that it may be evident to all the world, that there are Christians, and societies of Christians, who hold the doctrine of the Trinity in as much abhorrence as they themselves can do.[123]

As fair-minded as this sounds, we must remember that Priestley aimed not to preserve the independent dignity of Judaism, but to convince Jews to convert to Unitarianism. Priestly was an adamant millenarian, confident that the arrival of the kingdom of God was close at hand and, like the Puritans, that it would be marked by the mass conversion of Jews to Christianity. It is significant, then, that he appended an "Address to the Jews" to his most famous work of comparative religion, *A Comparison of the Institutions of Moses with Those of the Hindoos and Other Ancient Nations*. The work explains the falseness of non-Christian religions, and the closing address urges Jews to understand their errors and accept their role in bringing about the Christian end times.

One might think that such an attitude could not have persisted past Priestley's day. And yet, as Arthur Versluis so convincingly argues in *American Transcendentalism and Asian Religions*, the Transcendentalists also held millenarian views. While not as explicitly Christian as Priestley, the Transcendentalists nonetheless also anticipated a period of hitherto unimaginable progress and deep understanding. Moreover, this period would be recognizable by the Jews' adoption of Transcendentalism's own liberal, post-Christian position.[124] The belief persisted throughout late nineteenth-century Unitarianism, as formal and informal connections grew between Unitarians and Reform Jews. Reform rabbis and Unitarian ministers exchanged pulpits and shared a common hope for "the imminent arrival of a 'religion of humanity' characterized by the belief in the Fatherhood of God and the Brotherhood of Man."[125] But this agreement, as broad as it was, eventually proved divisive.

Rabbi Israel Wise considered Unitarians and Jews "spiritual cousins," and he established relationships with leading Unitarians. In his memoirs, he recalls meeting Daniel Webster in 1852, and how the two men agreed that "there was no essential difference in the matter of doctrine [between Reform Jews and Unitarians], but [only] in historical development."[126] This shared understanding moved Webster to remark that "we are all Unitarians," which highlighted the central point of contention between the two movements. For while both Reform Jews and Unitarians looked forward to a day of religious universalism, each continued to see itself as the only logical host for that universalism. So while at first it seemed a great concession to say that only "historical development" separated the two traditions, those differences in historical development soon came to mean everything. Rabbi Wise served on the board of the Free Religious Association, which deliberately recruited Jews, and he was deeply shocked when he realized that many of the Unitarians in the association, although they did not identify as Christians, nonetheless believed that the Christian revelation and experience had superseded the Jewish one. For his part, Rabbi Wise believed that Moses's revelation was original and sufficient, and the hurtful clash of Unitarian and Reform Jewish triumphalism commenced.

Theological commonalities that both groups once celebrated became a threat, and all parties now needed to demonstrate their allegiance to their own side. This was most clearly demonstrated in 1886 when Rabbi Solomon Sonneschein visited the American Unitarian Association headquarters in order to explore the possibility of taking a Unitarian pulpit. The historian Benny Kraut, who explored this episode in depth, writes, "The contemptuous Jewish denunciations of [Rabbi Sonneschein's] action, and the varied sources from which they came, reveal much about the true limits of American Reform Judaism, which were demarcated as much by ethnic-communal concerns as by religious-theological ones."[127] The same could be said of Unitarianism at the time, which had not progressed much beyond James Freeman Clark's *Ten Great Religions* (1871). Clark argued for the universality of all world religions, yet went on to argue that liberal Christianity best captures that universality.

A partnership between Unitarianism and Judaism that arose in the years between the world wars around Frederic Melcher, a Unitarian layperson and publisher, had almost the opposite effect; it created a shared cultural space while diminishing institutional religious commitments. Melcher initiated a liberal interfaith committee that met in the fall of 1920 to develop plans for an annual Religious Book Week. This promotion of religious books not only employed the traditional tools of the market but unleashed a new kind of sales force in the largely unwitting form of respected public figures, libraries, women's groups, denominational journals, and congregations themselves. Melcher and other publishers had learned much earlier that their most successful advertising promoted reading in general rather than the purchase of specific titles. It was easy to get clergy, politicians, and librarians to speak publicly about the virtues of morally uplifting reading; such statements did not feel like unseemly commercial advertising. And the clergy happily claimed the role of expert guides to thoughtful choices and pious reading strategies with the expanded market. Books mentioned from the pulpit sold well, and before long congregations even hosted publishers' book displays. Producing religious books for middle-class American audiences had become big business, and reading them became—even more than church-going—a central component of engaged religious life.

But more central to our story is how the books included in Religious Book Week expanded beyond the confines of Protestantism. After the Second World War, the federal government asked the National Council of Christians and Jews to help promote "Judeo-Christian" values as the core of American culture—a deliberate attempt to reclaim Christianity from fascist appropriation and Nazi anti-Semitism. Melcher's Religious Book Week proved perfect for this purpose. The titles it promoted now included not only the usual liberal Protestant works, based on individuals' inner spiritual experience, but Jewish and Catholic works as well. Religious publishing became broader and more cosmopolitan than churches and conventional attitudes had prescribed. The effect on American culture was enormous, as Matthew Hedstrom documents in *The Rise of Liberal Religion*:

> From the broadening impulses of the Religious Book Club and Religious Book Week and the mass interfaith appeal of [titles such as Joshua] Liebman's *Peace of Mind* and [Thomas] Merton's *Seven Storey Mountain*, one can readily comprehend the move in postwar popular religious culture to Jack Kerouac and George Harrison and later to Deepak Chopra, the immense celebrity of the Dalai Lama, and the ubiquitous yoga centers, full of Jewish and Protestant and Catholic seekers, in strip malls across America.[128]

Ironically, though, Melcher's very success reveals the degree to which the liberal religious establishment itself created the comfortably interfaith, "spiritual but not religious" Americans it would come to deride for their individualism, consumerist eclecticism, and lack of commitment to religious institutions.

CONCLUSION

Being itself is given to us as meaning. Being does not have meaning. Being itself, the phenomenon of Being, is meaning that is, in turn, its own circulation—and we are this circulation.

There is no meaning if meaning is not shared, and not because there would be an ultimate or first signification that all beings have in common, but because meaning is itself the sharing of Being. . . .

If one can put it like this, there is no other meaning than the meaning of circulation. But this circulation goes in all directions at once, in all the directions of all the space-times opened by presence to presence: all things, all beings, all entities, everything past and future, alive, dead, inanimate, stones, plants, nails, gods—and "humans."

—Jean Luc Nancy, *Being Singular Plural*

I believe that the increasing presence of Jews and Muslims in our congregations, as well as the anti-racist work that we have done and of which we have so much left to do, is both the result and the cause of hopeful fractures in our unhelpful allegiance to a long-moribund social location. I hope that we will more fully claim the multi-religious aspect of our identity. Not because the conversion of Jews and Muslims would be a triumph for us, not even because claiming multi-religiosity might allow us to escape our identity neurosis (although I pray that it will); but because, in doing so, we will finally realize that it is impossible to serve justice, let alone the God shared by Jews, Christians, and Muslims, without the very same staggering and reeling that the Puritans had warned would result from straying from singular and official truths. I hope that the good news will be that we have no further to stagger and reel than into our own collective past.

I conclude with a final story about interfaith engagement, multi-religious promise, and religious identity. In 1990 Rabbi Zallman M. Schacter-Shalomi, one of the founders of the Jewish Renewal movement, took part in a Jewish delegation that met with the Dalai Lama, at his request, in his exile community in India. Knowing that his Tibetan Buddhist community could not return to a Tibet controlled by communist China without facing extreme persecution, the Dalai Lama wondered how his people could maintain their religious identity in diaspora. He figured the Jews would understand this difficulty like no others. Indeed, one of the delegation said, only somewhat in jest, something like "they should only think to ask us this now!" The Jewish delegation, initially somewhat confused and embarrassed by the number of Jews who had left Judaism for Buddhism, came to realize they could also learn a lesson from the Tibetans. When the Jewish delegation asked the Dalai Lama why so many Jews converted to Buddhism, he charged them with renewing their own spiritual practices and making them vibrant for a new generation. This provided new momentum and encouragement to the Jewish Renewal Movement.[129]

As someone much concerned with Unitarian Universalist identity, I have wondered what unique and precious elements of our heritage one might travel to the UUA's headquarters to receive. Probably not a lesson about spiritual renewal or living in diaspora, unless we mean diaspora from Boston. And as much as I love Unitarian Universalism, I have to admit that until recently, those on such a pilgrimage were likely to be disappointed. Until April 2014, the UUA's headquarters stood at 25 Beacon Street in Boston, next to the magnificent Massachusetts State House with its impressive gold dome. First-time visitors often mistook the statehouse for the headquarters, because it looks like something befitting the seat of a denomination, only to be seriously disappointed when they found the poorly aging brownstone next door. To find the precious gifts we might offer, they had to enter our unprepossessing front door, climb our dark paneled staircase, and make it past the portraits of our well-dressed dead. As I write, the UUA is moving to a new home, partly in an attempt to break with the more exclusivist aspects of our past. Yet what Unitarian Universalism has always understood, even if cultural values have sometimes kept it from acting on that understanding, is that religion is not a container, but a matrix of relationships. Religion is not a single thing, nor is it ever the same. It is not a substance, it is an action. And if religion is relationship, then it is inherently multi-religious. Not only because, as Jean-Luc Nancy says,[130] there has always been a previous acculturation, although there has been; not only because no religion has a pure and simple origin; but because at a deep level religion is itself a mixed gesture—or, better yet, a mixing gesture.

NOTES

1   Wilbur, *A History of Unitarianism,* 2:164–65; see also Cadzow, Ludanyi, and Elteto, *Transylvania.*

2   Balázs, *Early Transylvanian Anti-Trinitarianism,* 147.

3   Hughes, "Who Really Said That?"

4   Kratochvil, "The Influence of Islam in Transylvania."

5   On the lack of government documents, see Péter, "Tolerance and Intolerance." On the denial of connections, see Kratochvil, "The Influence of Islam in Transylvania."

6   Daniel Boyarin's *Border Lines* is my guide here, not only on how the religious traditions that develop along borderlines are especially interesting for study, but also on how religions only develop on borders.

7   "Borders themselves are not given but constructed by power to mask hybridity, to occlude and disown it. The localization of hybridity in some others, called hybrids or heretics, serves that purpose." Boyarin, *Border Lines,* 15.

8   Bloom, foreword to Menocal, *Ornament of the World.*

9   Chittick, *Imaginal Worlds.*

10 Rubenstein, *When Jesus Became God*, 260. It is confusing that Rubenstein uses the non-ancient name "Jehovah" here, the Latinization of the Hebrew proper name for God that is often rendered as Yahweh.

11 Yuval, "Easter and Passover."

12 Percival, *The Seven Ecumenical Councils*, 54.

13 Armstrong, *Muhammad*, 159.

14 Serjeant, "The *Sunnah Jami'ah*," 4.

15 Khan, "The Medina Constitution," 3.

16 Armstrong, *Muhammad*, 15.

17 Not all Christian martyrs in ninth-century Cordova were condemned for behavior as aggressive as Perfectus's. Overall, forty-eight Christians were killed in this period for capital crimes against Islamic law. Coope, *The Martyrs of Córdoba*.

18 Boyarin, *Border Lines*, xiv.

19 Ibid., xvi.

20 Asad, *Genealogies of Religion*; Boyarin, "Semantic Differences."

21 See, for example, Waldman, "Commandment the First."

22 Duchesne, *Early History of the Christian Church*, 2:456.

23 Barnes and Williams, introduction to *Arianism after Arius*, xiii–xvii.

24 Cleland, "Islam and Unitarians."

25 Lyman, "A Topography of Heresy."

26 Wilbur, "How the History Came to Be Written."

27 Goring, "Unitarianism."

28 Wilbur, "The Meaning and Lesson of Unitarian History."

29 Wilbur, *Our Unitarian Heritage*, 52.

30 Brakke, "Jewish Flesh and Christian Spirit."

31 Shepardson, "Exchanging Reed for Reed."

32 *The Jewish Encyclopedia*, s.v. "Arianism."

33 Described in Menocal, *Ornament of the World,* 49.

34 See Meyerson, *The Muslims of Valencia.*

35 Perry, "Behind the Veil."

36 "Women went to great lengths to hide forbidden books in their clothing, usually in their bodice or between their legs, with the result that inquisitorial searches can be considered a sort of symbolic violation of the female bodies that sought to protect those writings. . . . Morisco women demonstrated an almost visceral relationship with written texts and created for themselves a crucial role as the guardians of Islamic tradition." Surtz, "Morisco Women," 421.

37 Baron, *The Ottoman Empire, Persia, Ethiopia, India and China,* 132.

38 Examples of this claim include Frederickson, *Racism,* and Hannaford, *Race.* I like María Elena Martínez's view, based on her comparison of ideas of blood purity in Spain with those that emerged in colonial Mexico, that "there is no single, transhistorical racism but different types of racisms, each produced by specific social and historical conditions." Martínez, *Genealogical Fictions,* 11.

39 Friedman, *Michael Servetus,* 129.

40 Popkin, "Beginnings of Modern Anti-Trinitarianism."

41 *De trinitatis errobus,* 42b–43a, 56b, cited in Bainton, *Hunted Heretic,* 8.

42 The conscious efforts of these men to establish Unitarianism are discussed by Massimo Firpo in *Antitrinitari nell'Europa orientale de '500;* see the review by Anne Jacobson Schutte in *Renaissance Quarterly.*

43 Schaeffer, review of *Disputatio scholastica,* by Iacobus Palaeologous.

44 Goodwin, *Lords of the Horizons,* 86.

45 Cadzow, Ludanyi, and Elteto, *Transylvania.*

46 Wilbur: *A History of Unitarianism: Transylvania, England, and America,* 22.

47 Quoted in Wilbur, *A History of Unitarianism,* 1:203.

48 Balázs, *Early Transylvanian Anti-Trinitarianism,* 37.

49 Such a claim is made in Forsey, *Queen Isabella . . . and Sultan Suleyman,* 117. One key source for the claim that Isabella's edict was a precedent for the Edict of Torda was Earl Morse Wilbur's 1925 *Our Unitarian Heritage.* Wilbur, however, corrects his mistake in the second volume of *A History of Unitarianism* (p. 22), noting that Queen Isabella was not interested in toleration per se, and that her proclamation of 1557 outlawed the growing Sacramentarian movement.

50 See, for example, Unghváry, *The Hungarian Protestant Reformation.*

51 Williams, *The Radical Reformation,* 1105.

52 *Islam: Empire of Faith.*

53 Sugar, *Southeastern Europe under Ottoman Rule,* 5; Inalcik, "Foundations of Ottoman-Jewish Cooperation." For an account of how earlier *dhimma* law was incorporated and practiced by the Ottomans, see Gibb and Bowen, *Islamic Society and the West,* esp. 211–12.

54 Inalcik, "Foundations of Ottoman-Jewish Cooperation," 7.

55 "In the long run Ottoman Jewry learned to live with an increased variety of groups and approaches and, perhaps because of that plurality, was able to develop an even more flourishing and pulsating cultural life." Baron, *The Ottoman Empire, Persia, Ethiopia, India and China,* 42.

56 Braude and Lewis, *Christian and Jews in the Ottoman Empire.*

57 Béla, "The Connection," 142.

58 Unitarianism, for example, is often referred to in the nationalistic lit-

erature as being uniquely suited to the spirit of the Hungarian people. While this association occurs most frequently in the literature of Hungarian Unitarians, it is interesting to note the degree to which many modern American Unitarians maintain the connection. See Stephen Sisa, *The Spirit of Hungary* (New Jersey: Vista Books, 1990), 86.

59 Unghváry, *The Hungarian Protestant Reformation*, 334, referring to Wilbur, *A Unitarian History*, 45.

60 Gunny, *Images of Islam*, 78.

61 Compier, "'Let the Muslim Be My Master.'"

62 Two of my favorite stories of creative relationship between European Christendom and Islam are told about the siege of Vienna. According to one, Vienna's long love affair with coffee began when some townsmen slipped out of the city to see what the besiegers were eating and drinking; fascinated by the strange, dark beans, they brought some home with them. Vienna's bakers supposedly had a more hostile response to the Ottomans. Working in the early morning, they heard Ottoman soldiers attempting to dig under the city walls. After giving the alarm, they took to making pastries in the form of the crescent that symbolizes Islam. Eating croissants, then, was allegedly a way of signaling defiance. Food historians have easily disproved both legends, but I enjoy the creative cultural exchange they suggest.

63 Matar, "Toleration of Muslims in Renaissance England," 134.

64 Tihany, "Islam and the Eastern Frontiers."

65 Hunt, "Were Western European Women the Luckiest Women in the World?" 28.

66 Both the quotation and the story about the turban are from Paul Tharius's 1613 "Idea Christianorum Hungarorum in et sub Turcismo." Farkas was a Lutheran clergyman, a rector at the reformed

theological school in Tolna. He hoped to stir up anti-Ottoman and pro-Habsburg sentiment amongst Protestants living in areas controlled by the Habsburgs. Quoted in Tihany, "Islam and the Eastern Frontiers," 58.

67   For example, Tihany, "Islam and the Eastern Frontiers"; Unghváry, *The Hungarian Protestant Reformation*.

68   The fascinating dynamic of "turning Turk" is explored in Vitkus, *Turning Turk*.

69   Murdock, *Calvinism on the Frontier*, 112.

70   Berkes, *The Development of Secularism*, 39.

71   Péter, "Tolerance and Intolerance," 360.

72   Imber, *The Ottoman Empire*, 134–35.

73   *Islam: Empire of Faith*.

74   Imber, *The Ottoman Empire*, 136.

75   Imber, *The Ottoman Empire*, 164.

76   Tihany, "Islam and the Eastern Frontiers," 55, citing Géza Kathona, *Fejezetek a török Hodoltsági reformáció történetéböl* (Budapest: Akadémiai Kiadó, 1974).

77   Bayerle, ed., *Letters of Ali Pasha*, vii–ix.

78   Kaufmann, *Das Ende der Reformation*, 291–92. I appreciate Abdul Haq Compier's pointing out this reference in private correspondence, Feb. 24, 2010.

79   Wilbur, *A History of Unitarianism*, 2:84–85.

80   Tihany, "Islam and the Eastern Frontiers."

81   Imber, *The Ottoman Empire*, 217.

82   Romania's HIV infection rates are among the highest in the world, partly because blood transfusions have often been used to treat starvation-related anemia. McNeil, "Romania's AIDS Children."

83 Gellérd, "Spiritual Jews of Szekler Jerusalem."

84 Popkin, "Beginnings of Modern Anti-Trinitarianism."

85 Bainton, *Hunted Heretic,* 64–65.

86 Schutte, review of *Antitrinitari nell'Europa orientale de '500,* by Massimo Firpo.

87 Rosenthal, "Marcin Czechowic and Jacob of Belzyce," 89.

88 Williams, *The Radical Reformation,* 871.

89 Ibid., 1265.

90 Pomogáts, "Jews by Choice."

91 As quoted and translated by Béla Pomogáts in "Jews by Choice."

92 Williams, *The Radical Reformation*, 1129.

93 Weltner, "A Place We Could Bring Our Jewishness."

94 Friedman, "Unitarians and New Christians," 238.

95 Erik Seeman has done fascinating work comparing clerical and lay attitudes toward death, work that suggests the laity were far more inclined to assume salvation than the clergy. See "She Died Like Good Old Jacob: Death Bed Scenes and Attitudes toward Death" in his *Pious Persuasions,* 44–78.

96 Hall, *Worlds of Wonder,* 138.

97 Mullen, "A Narrative of the Troubles."

98 Miller, "From Edwards to Emerson," 596.

99 Ibid., 596.

100 Howe, *The Unitarian Conscience,* 12.

101 On the tendency of middle class white persons to invent prosperous ancestors, see Thandeka, *Learning to Be White*, 51–56. On specifically Unitarian Universalist overstatements of affluence, see Thandeka, "What's Wrong with Anti-Racism?"

102 Buehrens, "Walking More Humbly."

103 Pierre Bourdieu has helpfully distinguished "cultural capital" from "economic capital." "Cultural capital" means the attributes, such as education, that allow a person to rise in social rank regardless of financial status. Bourdieu, "The Forms of Capital."

104 Douglas, "Clerical Disestablishment," "Feminine Disestablishment," and "Ministers and Mothers" in *The Feminization of American Culture;* Field, "The Birth of the Brahmins" and "Towards a Secular High Culture" in *The Crisis of the Standing Order;* Buell, "Unitarian Aesthetics."

105 Field, *The Crisis of the Standing Order,* 110.

106 De Benneville's story is told by Thandeka in "The Life of Small Group Ministries," from which the following description and quotations are taken.

107 Snyder, "The Religion of Humanity."

108 Versluis, *American Transcendentalism and Asian Religions,* 83.

109 For example, Mace, "Citizens of all the World's Temples."

110 "If one wants to fathom how the writer Coleman Barks has managed to turn Rumi into a best-selling poet in contemporary America, one would do well to place Alger's *Poetry of the East* alongside Barks's *The Soul of Rumi* and see their common wellsprings." Schmidt, *Restless Souls,* 82–83.

111 Quoted in Versluis, *American Transcendentalism and Asian Religions,* 149.

112 Quoted in ibid., 133.

113 On Webb, see Abd-Allah, *A Muslim in Victorian America.*

114 Schmidt, *Restless Souls,* 183, 182.

115 "The Fall of Islam in America: The Story of a Mussulman Propaganda That Came to Grief," *New York Times.*

116 Skinner, "The Good We Can Do."

117 Unitarian Universalist Association, *Unitarian Universalists and Islam,* 3.

118 Hertzberg, "The New England Puritans and the Jews."

119 Popkin, "The Jewish Indian Theory."

120 McKanan, *Identifying the Image of God;* Buchanan, "Tares in the Wheat."

121 Adams, *The Education of Henry Adams,* 3.

122 Ibid.

123 Quoted in Van den Berg, "Priestly, the Jews and the Millennium," 260.

124 Versluis, *American Transcendentalism and Asian Religion,* 176; 194; 307; 312.

125 Kraut, "Judaism Triumphant," 180. See also Kraut, "Ambivalent Relations"; Kraut, "A Unitarian Rabbi?"

126 Kraut, "Judaism Triumphant," 186.

127 Kraut, "A Unitarian Rabbi?" 308.

128 Hedstrom, *The Rise of Liberal Religion,* 224.

129 Kamenetz, *The Jew in the Lotus,* 1–16.

130 Nancy, *Being Singular Plural,* 152; see the epigraph with which I began this book.

BIBLIOGRAPHY

Abd-Allah, Umar F. *A Muslim in Victorian America: The Life of Alexander Russell Webb*. Oxford: Oxford University Press, 2006.

Adams, Henry. *The Education of Henry Adams*. Boston: Riverside Press for the Massachusetts Historical Society, 1918.

Armstrong, Karen. *Muhammad: A Biography of the Prophet*. San Francisco: HarperSanFrancisco, 1992.

Asad, Talal. *Genealogies of Religion: Discipline and Reasons of Power in Christianity and Islam*. Baltimore: Johns Hopkins University Press, 1993.

Bainton, Roland H. *Hunted Heretic: The Life and Death of Michael Servetus, 1511–1553*. Rev. ed. Providence, R.I.: Blackstone Editions, Unitarian Universalist Historical Society, 2005.

Balázs, Mihály. *Early Transylvanian Anti-Trinitarianism (1566–1571): From Servet to Palaeologus*. Translated by Gyorgy Novak. Biblioteca Dissidentium, Scripta et Studia 7. Baden-Baden: Editions Valentin Koerner, 1996.

Barnes, Michel, and Daniel H. Williams. Introduction to *Arianism after Arius: Essays on the Development of the Fourth Century Trinitarian Conflicts*, xiii–xvii. Edinburgh: T&T Clark, 1993.

Baron, Salo W. *The Ottoman Empire, Persia, Ethiopia, India and China*. Vol. 18 of *A Social and Religious History of the Jews*. New York: Columbia University Press, 1983.

Bayerle, Gustav, ed. *The Hungarian Letters of Ali Pasha of Buda, 1604–1616*. Budapest: Akadémiai Kiadó, 1991.

Béla, Mester. "The Connection between the Unitarian Thought and Early Modern Political Philosophy." *Journal of the Study of Religions and Ideologies* 1, no. 3 (winter 2002): 142–57.

Berkes, Niyazi. *The Development of Secularism in Turkey*. Montreal: McGill University Press, 1964.

Bourdieu, Pierre. "The Forms of Capital." In *Handbook of Theory and Research for the Sociology of Education*, edited by John G. Richardson, 241–58. New York: Greenwood, 1986.

Boyarin, Daniel. *Border Lines: The Partition of Judaeo-Christianity*. Philadelphia: University of Pennsylvania Press, 2004.

———. "Semantic Differences; or, 'Judaism'/'Christianity.'" In *The Ways That Never Parted: Jews and Christians in Late Antiquity and the Early Middle Ages*, edited by Adam H. Becker and Annette Yoshito Reed, 65–86. Minneapolis: Fortress, 2007.

Brakke, David. "Jewish Flesh and Christian Spirit in Athanasius of Alexandria." *Journal of Early Christian Studies* 9, no. 4 (winter 2001): 453–81.

Braude, Benjamin, and Bernard Lewis, eds. *Christians and Jews in the Ottoman Empire: The Functioning of a Plural Society*. New York: Holmes and Meier, 1982.

Buchanan, Daniel P. "Tares in the Wheat: Puritan Violence and Puritan Families in the Nineteenth Century Liberal Imagination." *Religion and American Culture* 8, no. 2 (summer 1998): 205–36.

Buehrens, John. "Walking More Humbly and Thriving." Minns lecture, Oak Park, Illinois, May 4, 2012.

Buell, Lawrence I. "Unitarian Aesthetics and Emerson's Poet Priest." *American Quarterly* 20, no. 1 (spring 1968): 3–20.

Cadzow, John F., Andrew Ludanyi, and Louis J. Elteto. *Transylvania: The Roots of Ethnic Conflict*. Kent, Ohio: Kent State University Press, 1983.

Chittick, William C. *Imaginal Worlds: Ibn al-'Arabī and the Problem of Religious Diversity*. Albany: State University of New York Press, 1994.

Clark, James Freeman. *Ten Great Religions: An Essay in Comparative Theology*. Boston: James R. Osgood, 1871.

Cleland, Bilal. "Islam and Unitarians—The Quest for Truth and Justice." An address to the congregation of the Unitarian Peace Memorial Church, Melbourne, Australia, Sunday, April 13, 2003. english.islammessage.com/ArticleDetails.aspx?articleId=1043.

Compier, Abdul Haq. "'Let the Muslim Be My Master in Outward Things': References to Islam in the Promotion of Religious Tolerance in Europe." Paper presented at the *Britain and the Muslim World* conference, Exeter University, April 17–19, 2009.

Coope, Jessica A. *The Martyrs of Códoba: Community and Family Conflict in an Age of Mass Conversion*. Lincoln: University of Nebraska Press, 1995.

Douglas, Ann. *The Feminization of American Culture*. New York: Noonday, 1998.

Duchesne, Louis. *Early History of the Christian Church: From Its Foundation to the End of the Fifth Century*. Ithaca: Cornell University Press, 2009.

"The Fall of Islam in America: The Story of a Mussulman Propaganda That Came to Grief." December 1, 1895, *New York Times*, http://query.nytimes.com/mem/archive-free/pdf?res=F4081E FA3A5D15738DDDA80894DA415B8585F0D3.

Field, Peter S. *The Crisis of the Standing Order: Clerical Intellectuals and Cultural Authority in Massachusetts, 1780–1833.* Amherst: University of Massachusetts Press, 1998.

Forsey, Alicia. *Queen Isabella Sforza Szapolyai of Transylvania and Sultan Suleyman of the Ottoman Empire: A Case of Sixteenth-Century Muslim-Christian Cooperation.* Lewiston, N.Y.: Edwin Mellon, 2009.

Fredrickson, George M. *Racism: A Short History.* Princeton, N.J.: Princeton University Press, 2002.

Friedman, Jerome. *Michael Servetus: A Case Study in Total Heresy.* Geneva: Librarie Droz S.A., 1978.

———."Unitarians and New Christians in Sixteenth-Century Europe." *Archiv für Reformationsgeschichte* 81 (1990): 216–38.

Gaskell, Elizabeth Cleghorn. *North and South.* 1855. Reprint, Oxford: Oxford University Press, 2008.

Gellérd, Judit. "Spiritual Jews of Szekler Jerusalem: A Four-Centuries History of Transylvanian Szekler Jerusalem." Unpublished paper. unitarius.uw.hu/cffr/papers/sabbat.htm.

Gibb, H. A. R., and Harold Bowen. *Islamic Society and the West.* London: Oxford University Press, 1950.

Goodwin, Jason. *Lords of the Horizons: A History of the Ottoman Empire.* New York: Henry Holt, 1999.

Goring, Jeremy. "Unitarianism: History, Myth, or Make-Believe." *Transactions of the Unitarian Historical Society* 19, no. 4 (1990): 213–27.

Gunny, Ahmad. *Images of Islam in Eighteenth-Century Writings.* London: Grey Seal, 1996.

Hall, David D. *Worlds of Wonder, Days of Judgment: Popular Religious Belief in Early New England.* Cambridge, Mass.: Harvard University Press, 1989.

Hannaford, Ivan. *Race: The History of an Idea in the West.* Washington, D.C.: Woodrow Wilson Center Press, 1996.

Hedstrom, Matthew S. *The Rise of Liberal Religion: Book Culture and American Spirituality in the Twentieth Century.* Oxford: Oxford University Press, 2013.

Hertzberg, Arthur. "The New England Puritans and the Jews." In *Hebrew and the Bible in America: The First Two Centuries,* edited by Shalom Goldmann, 105–22. Hanover, N.H.: University Press of New England, 1993.

Howe, Daniel Walker. *The Unitarian Conscience: Harvard Moral Philosophy, 1805–1861.* Middletown, Conn.: Wesleyan University Press, 1970.

Hughes, Peter. "Who Really Said That?" *UU World* 26, no. 3 (fall 2012): 52–54.

Hunt, Margaret R. "Were Western European Women the Luckiest Women in the World? Comparing the Status of Women in the Law Courts of Early Modern Western Europe and the Ottoman Empire." In *Proceedings of the Women in Early Modern Europe Annual Conference in Amherst,* unpublished, 2004.

Imber, Colin. *The Ottoman Empire, 1300–1650: The Structure of Power.* New York: Palgrave Macmillan, 2002.

Inalcik, Halil. "Foundations of Ottoman-Jewish Cooperation." In *Jews, Turks, Ottomans: A Shared History, Fifteenth through the Twentieth Century,* edited by Avigdor Levy, 3–14. Syracuse, N.Y.: Syracuse University Press, 2002.

Islam: Empire of Faith. DVD. Directed by Robert H. Gardner. London: BBC Documentary, 2003.

The Jewish Encyclopedia. 1901–6. www.jewishencyclopedia.com.

Kahn, Ali. "The Medina Constitution." *Understanding Islamic Law,* Social Science Research Network, 2006. papers.ssrn.com/sol3/papers.cfm?abstract_id=945458.

Kamenetz, Rodger. *The Jew in the Lotus: A Poet's Rediscovery of Jewish Identity in Buddhist India.* New York: HarperOne, 2007.

Kaufmann, Thomas. *Das Ende der Reformation: Magdeburgs "Herrgotts Kanzlei" (1548–1551/2).* Tubingen: Mohr Siebeck, 2003.

Khan, Ali. "The Medina Constitution." *Understanding Islamic Law,* 2006. Social Science Research Network. ssrn.com/abstract=945458.

Kratochvil, Naná. "The Influence of Islam in Transylvania: A Speculative Reconstruction." Paper presented to the Ohio River Study Group of Unitarian Universalist Ministers, Akron, Ohio, Oct. 5, 1999.

Kraut, Benny. "The Ambivalent Relations between American Reform Judaism and Unitarianism in the Last Third of the Nineteenth Century." *Journal of Ecumenical Studies* 23 (1986): 58–68.

———. "Judaism Triumphant: Isaac Mayer Wise on Unitarianism and Liberal Christianity." *American Jewish Studies Review* 7–8 (1982–83): 179–230.

———. "A Unitarian Rabbi? The Case of Solomon H. Sonneschein." In *Jewish Apostasy in the Modern World,* edited by Todd M. Endelman, 272–308. New York: Holmes & Meier, 1987.

Levenson, J. C. "The Etiology of Israel Adams: The Onset, Waning, and Relevance of Henry Adam's Anti-Semitism." *New Literary History* 25 (June 1994): 569–600.

Lyman, Rebecca. "A Topography of Heresy: Mapping The Rhetorical Creation of Arianism." In *Arianism after Arius: Essays on the Development of the Fourth-Century Trinitarian Conflicts*, edited by Michel Barnes and Daniel H. Williams, 45–64. Edinburgh: T&T Clark, 1993.

Mace, Emily. "Citizens of All the World's Temples: Cosmopolitan Religion at Bell Street Chapel." In *American Religious Liberalism*, edited by Leigh Schmidt and Sally Promey, 141–60. Bloomington: Indiana University Press, 2012.

Martínez, María Elena. *Genealogical Fictions: Limpieza de Sangre, Religion, and Gender in Colonial Mexico*. Stanford: Stanford University Press, 2008.

Matar, Nabil. *Europe through Arab Eyes, 1578–1727*. New York: Columbia University Press, 2009.

———. "The Toleration of Muslims in Renaissance England: Practice and Theory." In *Religious Toleration: The Variety of Rites from Cyrus to Defoe*, edited by John Christian Laursen, 127–46. London: Palgrave Macmillan, 1999.

Mather, Cotton. *Magnalia Christi americana: The Ecclesiastical History of New-England*. 1702. Reprint, Hartford, Conn.: Silas Andrus and Sons, 1885.

McKanan, Dan. *Identifying the Image of God: Radical Christians and Nonviolent Power in the Antebellum United States*. Oxford: Oxford University Press, 2002.

McNeil, Donald, Jr. "Romania's AIDS Children: A Lifeline Lost." *New York Times*, January 7, 2001.

Menocal, María Rosa. *The Ornament of the World: How Muslims, Jews, and Christians Created a Culture of Tolerance in Medieval Spain*. With a foreword by Harold Bloom. New York: Little, Brown, 2002.

Meyerson, Mark D. *The Muslims of Valencia in the Age of Fernando and Isabel: Between Coexistence and Crusade*. Berkeley: University of California Press, 1991.

Miller, Perry. "From Edwards to Emerson." *New England Quarterly* 13 (December 1940): 589–617.

Mullen, Lincoln A. "A Narrative of the Troubles in the Second Church in Windsor, 1735–1741." *Jonathan Edwards Studies* 2, no. 2 (2012): 83–97.

Murdock, Graeme. *Calvinism on the Frontier, 1600–1660: International Calvinism and the Reformed Church in Hungary and Transylvania*. Oxford: Oxford University Press, 2000.

Nancy, Jean-Luc. *Being Singular Plural*. Stanford: Stanford University Press, 2000.

Percival, Henry R., ed. *The Seven Ecumenical Councils of the Undivided Church*. Vol. 14. *The Nicene and Post-Nicene Fathers, Second Series*, Philip Schaff and Henry Wace, eds. New York: Charles Scribner's Sons, 1900.

Perry, Mary Elizabeth. "Behind the Veil: Moriscas and the Politics of Resistance and Survival." In *Spanish Women and the Golden Age: Images and Realities*, edited by Magdelena S. Sánchez and Alain Saint-Saëns, 37–53. Westport, Conn.: Greenwood, 1996.

Péter, Katalin. "Tolerance and Intolerance in Sixteenth-Century Hungary." In *Tolerance and Intolerance in the European Reformation*, edited by Ole Peter Grell and Bob Scribner, 249–61. Cambridge: Cambridge University Press, 1996.

Pomogáts, Béla. "Jews by Choice." *Hungarian Quarterly* 42, no. 164 (winter 2001).

Popkin, Richard H. "Marranos, New Christians, and the Beginnings of Modern Anti-Trinitarianism." In *Jews and Conversos at the Time of the Expulsion,* edited by Yom Tov Assis and Yosef Kaplan, 143–60. Jerusalem: The Zalman Shazar Center for Jewish History, 1999.

———. "The Rise and the Fall of the Jewish Indian Theory." In *Hebrew and the Bible in America: The First Two Centuries,* edited by Shalom Goldman, 61–69. Hanover, N.H.: University Press of New England, 1993.

Rosenthal, Judah M. "Marcin Czechowic and Jacob of Belzyce: Arian-Jewish Encounters in 16th Century Poland." *Proceedings of the American Academy of Jewish Research* 34 (1966): 77–97.

Rubenstein, Richard. *When Jesus Became God: The Struggle to Define Christianity during the Last Days of Rome.* Orlando, Fla.: Harcourt, 1999.

Schaeffer, Peter. Review of *Disputatio scholastica,* by Iacobus Palaeologous. *Sixteenth Century Journal* 27, no. 2 (summer 1996): 493–94.

Schmidt, Leigh Eric. *Restless Souls: The Making of American Spirituality from Emerson to Oprah.* New York: HarperCollins, 2005.

Schutte, Anne Jacobson. Review of *Antitrinitari nell'Europa orientale de '500: Nuovi testi di Szymon Budny, Niccolò Paruta e Iacopo Paleologo,* by Massimo Firpo. *Renaissance Quarterly* 33, no. 2 (summer 1980): 242–44.

Seeman, Erik. *Pious Persuasions: Laity and Clergy in Eighteenth-Century New England.* Baltimore: Johns Hopkins University Press, 1999.

Serjeant, R. B. "The *Sunnah Jami'ah,* Pacts with the Yathrib Jews, and the *Tahrim* of Yathrib: Analysis and Translation of the Documents Comprised in the So-Called 'Constitution of Medina.'" *Bulletin of the School of Oriental and African Studies* 41, no. 1 (February 1978): 1–42.

Shepardson, Christine C. "Exchanging Reed for Reed: Mapping Contemporary Heretics onto Biblical Jews in Ephrem's *Hymns on Faith.*" *Hugoye: Journal of Syriac Studies* 5, no. 1 (January 2002): 15–33. syrcom.cua.edu/Hugoye/Vol5No1/HV5N1Shepardson.html.

Sisa, Stephen. *The Spirit of Hungary: A Panorama of Hungarian History and Culture.* 2nd ed. Morristown, N.J.: Vista, 1990.

Skinner, Donald E. "The Good We Can Do: Responses from around the World." *UU World* 16, no. 1 (January/February 2002). www.uuworld.org/2002/01/feature3e.html.

Snyder, Lawrence. "The Religion of Humanity in Victorian America." In *Perspectives on American Religion and Culture*, edited by Peter Williams, 380–89. Oxford: Blackwell, 1999.

Sugar, Peter F. *Southeastern Europe under Ottoman Rule, 1354–1804.* Seattle: University of Washington Press, 1989.

Surtz, Ronald E. "Morisco Women, Written Texts, and the Valencia Inquisition." *Sixteenth Century Journal* 32, no. 2 (summer 2001): 421–33.

Thandeka. *Learning to Be White: Money, Race, and God in America.* New York: Continuum, 2000.

———. "The Life of Small Group Ministries." www.uua.org/documents/thandeka/life_sgm.pdf.

———. "What's Wrong with Anti-Racism?" Lecture at General Assembly, June, 1999. http://archive.uua.org/ga/ga99/238thandeka.html.

Tihany, Leslie C. "Islam and the Eastern Frontiers of Reformed Protestantism." *The Reformed Review: A Journal of the Seminaries of the Reformed Church in America* (Holland Michigan Western Theological School) 29 (1975): 52–71.

Unghváry, Alexander Sándor. *The Hungarian Protestant Reformation in the Sixteenth Century under the Ottoman Impact.* Lewiston, N.Y.: Edwin Mellen, 1989.

Unitarian Universalist Association. Washington Office for Advocacy. *Unitarian Universalists and Islam: An Introduction to Interfaith Dialogue and Reading Group Guide.* 2008. www.uusc.org/ buildingbridges/toolkit.

Van den Berg, J. "Priestly, the Jews and the Millennium." In *Sceptics, Millenarians and Jews,* edited by David S. Katz and Jonathan I. Israel, 256–74. Leiden: E. J. Brill, 1990.

Versluis, Arthur. *American Transcendentalism and Asian Religions.* New York: Oxford University Press, 1993.

Vitkus, Daniel J. *Turning Turk: English Theater and the Multicultural Mediterranean, 1570–1630.* New York: Palgrave Macmillan, 2003.

Waldman, Steve. "Commandment the First: Do Muslims and Christians Worship the Same God?" *Slate Magazine*, Dec. 17, 2013. http://www.slate.com/articles/life/faithbased/2003/12/commandment_the_first.html.

Weltner, Linda R. "A Place We Could Bring Our Jewishness." In *Discovering Unitarian Universalism from Catholic and Jewish Perspectives,* by Patrick T. O'Neill and Linda R. Weltner. Pamphlet. Boston: Unitarian Universalist Association, 1995. www.uua.org/ beliefs/welcome/judaism/151246.shtml.

Wilbur, Earl Morse. *A History of Unitarianism.* 2 vols. Cambridge, Mass.: Harvard University Press, 1945–52.

———. "How the History Came to Be Written." *Proceedings of the Unitarian Historical Society* 1951: 5–23.

———. "The Meaning and Lesson of Unitarian History." *Transactions of the Unitarian Historical Society* 3, no. 4 (1926): 350–60.

———. *Our Unitarian Heritage.* Boston: Beacon, 1925.

Williams, George Huntson. *The Radical Reformation.* 3rd ed. Kirksville, Mo.: Sixteenth Century Journal Publishers, 1992.

Yuval, Israel J. "Easter and Passover as Early Jewish-Christian Dialogue." In *Passover and Easter: Origin and History to Modern Times*, edited by Paul F. Bradshaw and Lawrence A. Hoffman, 98–124. Notre Dame, Ind.: University of Notre Dame Press, 1999.

ACKNOWLEDGMENTS

I am very grateful to the Minns Lecture Committee, the Starr King School for the Ministry, and my beloved home congregation in Lewis Center, Ohio, for supporting me in multiple ways as I pursued the questions and ideas that gave rise to this book.

I have benefitted from the interest of too many fine teachers, mentors, ministers, scholars, and friends to name. I am especially indebted to Amy Shuman, my most generous mentor, whose mind pushes beyond every border. The specific content of this book originated with discussions over the tennis net with Victoria Holbrook, the incomparably subtle scholar of all things Ottoman.

May this work convey my desire to offer a special blessing on all Jewish- and Muslim-identified persons who participate in and with Unitarian Universalist gatherings, and to all who have articulated and embodied the most radically hospitable forms of our faith.

Finally, I dedicate this and everything to my spouse Donna DeGeorge, because to make one out of two is to heal the wound of human nature.

INDEX

Abraham, Isaac ben, 47
Adams, Henry, 66–67
al-Andalus. *See* Andalusia
Alvinczi, George, 33–34
American Transcendentalism and Asian Religions (Versluis), 68
American Unitarianism. *See* North American Unitarianism
Andalusia, multiculturalism of, xii, xix–xx
anti-Islamic propaganda, 28–30
anti-Judaism, 2, 12, 15. *See also* anti-Semitism
Antinomianism, 56–57, 62
anti-Semitism, xx, 2, 12, 13, 15, 26, 39–40, 67
anti-Trinitarianism, xviii, 12, 13, 15–18, 23, 30–31, 40–43, 45, 52

An Appeal to the Serious and Candid Professors of Christianity (Priestly), 67–68
Aragon, Muslims in (1526), 14
Arians/Arianism, 6–9, 12–13, 51
Ariomaniacs, 9
Arius (Bishop), 6–11
Arminianism, 51–52
Arminius, Jacob, 51–52
Armstrong, Karen, 4
Asura (Muslim fast day), 3
Athanasius, 6, 8–9, 12

Balázs, Mihály, 23–24
Baron, Salo, 26
Being Singular Plural (Nancy), xiii, 73
Belzyce, Poland, 37
ben Hadou, Mohammad, 28
Berkes, Niyazi, 30–31